THE 𝕳artford 𝕮ourant AT 250

TELLING CONNECTICUT'S STORIES

The Moments That Make Up Our State's Richly Textured History

FOUNDED IN 1764

250 ♥ YEARS
Hartford Courant
A TRIBUNE PUBLISHING COMPANY

Richard J. Daniels, *Publisher and CEO* • **Andrew S. Julien,** *Vice President/Editor* • **Christine W. Taylor,** *Digital Editor*

ACKNOWLEDGMENTS

The work of thousands of writers, editors, photographers, cartoonists and graphic designers has enriched the pages of The Hartford Courant for 250 years. Throughout 2014 The Courant produced hundreds of stories, special sections, photo galleries, videos, quizzes and other features in print and online, highlighting Connecticut's remarkable history and the newspaper's coverage of it, and marking an anniversary no other newspaper in America has ever achieved.

This book was compiled and edited by Nancy Schoeffler, distilled from the work of numerous people, including John Adamian, John Altavilla, Daniela Altimari, Dave Altimari, Dom Amore, Mike Anthony, Susan Campbell, Ryan Cane, Jenna Carlesso, Suzanne Carlson, Tom Condon, Desmond Conner, Matthew Conyers, Shawn Courchesne, Steve Courtney, Sandra Csizmar, Bernard Davidow, Paul Doyle, David Drury, Susan Dunne, Anne Farrow, Jenifer Frank, Kenneth R. Gosselin, Steve Grant, Alaine Griffin, Dan Haar, Naedine Hazell, Erik Hesselberg, Gregory B. Hladky, Christopher Hoffman, Matthew Kauffman, Christopher Keating, Joel Lang, Jesse Leavenworth, Edmund H. Mahony, Peter Marteka, Owen McNally, Steve Metcalf, Joseph F. Nunes, Jeff Otterbein, David Owens, Scott Powers, Lori Riley, Frank Rizzo, Jim Shea, Peter Sleight, Julie Stagis, Matthew Sturdevant and Tom Yantz.

It also features pictures by current and former Courant photographers, including Tony Bacewicz, Harry Batz, Tom Brown, Tia Ann Chapman, Albert Dickson, Stephen Dunn, Mary Alice Dwyer, Al Ferreira, Robert B. Ficks, Judy Griesedieck, Dan Haar, Kathy Hanley, Bettina Hansen, Rick Hartford, Arman G. Hatsian, Kirk Hatsian, Brad Horrigan, Art Kiely Jr., Michael Kodas, Joanne HoYoung Lee, Michael Lennahan, John Long, Bob MacDonnell, Michael McAndrews, Richard Mei, Richard Messina, Mark Mirko, Maurice Murray, Cloe Poisson, Cecilia Prestamo, Anacleto Rapping, Patrick Raycraft, Marc Yves Regis I, Steve Silk, Shana Sureck, Joe Tabacca, Ross Taylor, Arthur Warmsley, Jerry Williams, John Woike and Dennis Yonan.

The Hartford Courant is particularly grateful to the staff of the Connecticut Historical Society for their generous assistance with research and images.

Special thanks as well to former Courant Publisher Nancy A. Meyer.

Book Editing – *Nancy Schoeffler*

Photo Editing and Research – *Sandra Csizmar; Naedine Hazell, Richard Messina, Cloe Poisson* • **Art Direction and Cover Design** – *Chris Moore*

FOREWORD

*"Of all the Arts which have been introduc'd amongst Mankind, for the civilizing Human-Nature,
and rendering Life agreeable and happy, none appear of greater Advantage than that of Printing; for hereby the greatest Genius's of
all Ages, and Nations, live and speak for the Benefit of future Generations."*

So declared Thomas Green in the first issue of The Connecticut Courant, which he printed on Oct. 29, 1764, at the Heart & Crown near the North Meeting House in Hartford.

Green probably never imagined that those "future generations" still would be reading his newspaper two and a half centuries later or that they would be reading it on computers, tablets and mobile phones. Yet on Oct. 29, 2014, The Hartford Courant celebrated 250 years of uninterrupted publication.

The Courant's legacy of journalism is older than the United States, older than the First Amendment's guarantee of a free press.

From the American Revolution to the digital revolution,

The Courant has chronicled wars, the inauguration of every president, scientific advances, natural disasters. We've seen long-held prejudices wither in the face of demands for change. We've been witness to unspeakable tragedies — at a circus fire in Hartford, at an elementary school in Newtown.

The many moments that have made up our richly textured history include more personal events as well — the first day of school, a soldier's return home, the tug of war over a town's budget, hard-fought games, religious rituals, holiday celebrations.

The tools and storytelling techniques have evolved and continue to evolve in the 21st century's increasingly complex and fast-paced media landscape. But The Hartford Courant's bedrock principles endure — a dedication to tirelessly seek truth and share knowledge, a devotion to excellence and accuracy, and a commitment to unite and strengthen our community by nurturing a deeper understanding of the people and events that shape it.

The Connecticut Courant.

MONDAY, OCTOBER 29, 1764. (Number co.)

HARTFORD: Printed by THOMAS GREEN, at the Heart and Crown, near the North-Meeting-House.

Hartford, October 29th, 1764.

OF all the Arts which have been introduc'd amongst Mankind, for the civilizing Human-Nature, and rendering Life agreeable and happy, none appear of greater Advantage than that of Printing ; for hereby the greatest Genius's of all Ages, and Nations, live and speak for the Benefit of future Generations.—

Was it not for the Press, we should be left almost intirely ignorant of all those noble Sentiments which the Antients were endow'd with.

By this Art, Men are brought acquainted with each other, though never so remote, as to Age or Situation; it lays open to View, the Manners, Genius and Policy of all Nations and Countries, and faithfully transmits them to Posterity —But not to insist upon the Usefulness of this Art in general, which must be obvious to every One, whose Thoughts are the least extensive.

The Benefit of a Weekly Paper, must in particular have its Advantages, as it is the Channel which conveys the History of the present Times to every Part of the World.

The Articles of News from the different Papers (which we shall receive every Saturday, from the neighbouring Provinces, that shall appear to us, to be most authentic and interesting shall always be carefully inserted ; and great Care will be taken to collect from Time to Time all domestic Occurrences, that are worthy the Notice of the Publick; for which, we shall always be obliged to any of our Correspondents, within whose Knowledge they may happen.

Front cover, clockwise from upper left:

Viola Bechard is consoled by Ernest Kosswig of the East Farmington Volunteer Fire Department after learning that her 7-year-old daughter had been swept to her death by floodwaters in Farmington during the August 1955 flood.
Robert B. Ficks / Hartford Courant

These soldiers from Connecticut's 26th Regiment were among those who served at the Civil War battle in Port Hudson, Louisiana, in 1863.
Middlesex County Museum and Historical Society

Katharine Hepburn receives a Red Cross campaign button from former Hartford Mayor Walter E. Batterson after she made a radio appeal for Red Cross donations at WTIC in Hartford in December 1941.
Harry Batz / Hartford Courant

The Hartford skyline is visible from Wickham Park in Manchester in October 2013.
John Woike / Hartford Courant

Back cover, from left:

Horses cart snow to dump in the Park River in Hartford after the Blizzard of 1888.
William H. Lockwood / Connecticut State Library

Smoke billows from the Ringling Bros. and Barnum & Bailey Circus big top in Hartford on July 6, 1944, in a fire that killed 168 people, many of them children.
Courant file photo

President Lyndon Baines Johnson shakes the hands of hundreds of admirers who reach through a large iron fence on Prospect Street as he campaigns in downtown Hartford in September 1964.
Robert B. Ficks / Hartford Courant

TABLE OF CONTENTS

Place

Hartford: The Heart Of Connecticut **6**

The Landscape: Our Changing Scenery **28**

Community: The Places We Call Home **40**

Public Life

War And Valor: Answering The Call **66**

Politics: The Constitution State **78**

Equal Rights: Breaking Down Barriers **92**

Challenges

Weather: Our Stormy History **104**

Crime: Law And Disorder **120**

Resiliency: Tragedy And Recovery **134**

Endeavors

State Of The Arts: Our Starring Roles **146**

Sports: Spirit Of Competition **164**

Innovation: Yankee Ingenuity **182**

Sponsors **194**

Index **204**

Left: Asylum Street at Ford and High streets in Hartford, circa 1924. *The Connecticut Historical Society*

THE HEART OF CONNECTICUT

Hartford's modern history began four centuries ago, in 1614, when Dutch explorer Adriaen Block sailed up the Connecticut River — in a region the Native Americans called Quinnehtukqut, meaning "beside the long, tidal river." By 1633, the Dutch established a fur trading post along the river in the area still known as Dutch Point.

That same year, Puritan preacher Thomas Hooker fled England for the Massachusetts Bay Colony, but he quickly chafed under the anti-Democratic views of the colony's governor, John Winthrop Sr. In 1636, encouraged by promising reports about the fertile Connecticut River valley, Hooker and the Rev. Samuel Stone led their parishioners west and established three settlements: Hartford, Wethersfield and Windsor.

The English settlers prospered: The river teemed with fish, including bountiful spring runs of shad and Atlantic salmon, and the rich soil of its flood plains was ideal for agriculture.

More than a century later, in 1764, printer Thomas Green opened his shop in Hartford, by then a growing port town with a population of about 4,000. The Courant's coverage of the Revolutionary War was considered so important that in 1778, when the local paper mill burned, the legislature authorized a lottery to raise funds to build a new one.

Commerce in Hartford continued to pick up. The riverfront was crowded with docks, wharves and shipyards. In 1792 the Hartford Bank opened for business. In 1794, the firm of Sanford and Wadsworth wrote its first fire insurance policy. And by 1796 the State House was completed.

Left: "The View of Hartford as Seen from East Hartford," oil on canvas, signed A.R.W., circa 1830-1850. The painting shows the Hartford Covered Bridge, which was built over the Connecticut River in 1818 and burned on May 17, 1895, and a cityscape that includes three prominent church steeples and smoke rising from four factory chimneys.
The Connecticut Historical Society

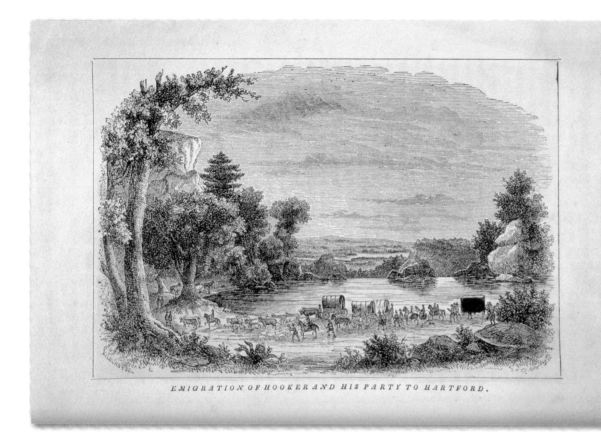

EMIGRATION OF HOOKER AND HIS PARTY TO HARTFORD.

Hooker's Company reach the Connecticut.

Above left: "Emigration of Hooker and His Party to Hartford," by Seth H. Clark, 1850s.
The Connecticut Historical Society

Above right: "Hooker's Company Reach the Connecticut."
"History of Middlesex County, Massachusetts" (1880, Vol. 1) by Samuel Adams Drake

Below right: Drawing of Thomas Hooker's house in Hartford, circa 1836. *The Connecticut Historical Society*

Opposite: "Reverend Thomas Hooker and Company Journeying Through the Wilderness in 1636 from Plymouth to Hartford" by Frederic Edwin Church, 1846. The painting's title contains a factual error: Hooker led his flock from Cambridge, Mass., not Plymouth. *Wadsworth Atheneum Museum of Art, Hartford*

COMING OF AGE

B
y the mid-1800s, Hartford was coming into its own as a city, pulsing with energy. The state Constitutional Convention in 1818 had disestablished the Congregational Church as the official religion, a major step toward religious tolerance just as waves of immigrants began to arrive.

The insurance industry had begun to develop, the railroad had arrived, and city leaders started to establish institutions like colleges, hospitals and an art museum.

And by 1820 the city had 20 publishing houses, publishing more books than in any other American city at the time.

Above left: The Old State House, 1834 drawing and watercolor by Edward Williams Clay. *The Connecticut Historical Society*

Above right: First Company Governor's Foot Guard, Hartford, at the Old State House, lithograph by E.B. & E.C. Kellogg, circa 1846-1852. *The Connecticut Historical Society*

Above left: The Wadsworth Atheneum, lithograph by E.B. & E.C. Kellogg, circa 1842-1848. The Atheneum was designed by Ithiel Town and Alexander Jackson Davis in the Gothic revival style. The gable is inscribed with the date 1842. *The Connecticut Historical Society*

Above right: In 1841, Daniel Wadsworth, an amateur artist and son of wealthy merchant Jeremiah Wadsworth, donated his plot of land on Main Street and $6,500 for the construction of what is now recognized as the country's first public art museum. A fundraising campaign raised $30,000. Wadsworth also raised $1,500 to buy more than 50 paintings from the American Academy of the Fine Arts in New York, which was folding. *Oil painting by Thomas Sully, 1807 / Wadsworth Atheneum Museum of Art*

Opposite: The state Capitol dome under construction, circa 1878. Architect Richard M. Upjohn, who had experience designing academic and ecclesiastical buildings but had never designed a government structure, first proposed putting a steeple atop the Capitol and then a clock tower. But the public insisted on a dome, and the design was changed during construction. *The Connecticut Historical Society*

Above: The Park River and the Soldiers and Sailors Memorial Arch, circa 1890. The river — earlier known as the Little River, the Mill River, the Hog River and, as Mark Twain sometimes called it, the Meandering Swine — ran through Bushnell Park and frequently flooded. *The Connecticut Historical Society*

Above right: Laundry hangs across the Park River in the area that fronted on Sheldon Street, looking west from Main Street, circa 1905. The state Capitol is seen in the background.
The Connecticut Historical Society

Below right: In 1942, the Park River was diverted through underground culverts along Elm Street to the Connecticut River. The small pond in Bushnell Park is part of the river's former path. *Hartford Courant archives*

CAPITAL CITY

T he city's ascendancy as a prosperous manufacturing center was in full flower by the latter half of the 19th century. The Colt Armory and a profusion of factories in the Frog Hollow neighborhood created a robust and complex economy, turning out rifles, sewing machines, bicycles and typewriters. In 1875, after 174 years of sharing the honor with New Haven, Hartford became the sole state capital.

Above: A lithograph of Hartford in 1879 shows a densely packed city, a steam locomotive, the state Capitol at right and the Park River looping around Bushnell Park and under a stone bridge. *The Connecticut Historical Society*

Opposite: The Connecticut Courant moved to this building on State Street in 1880. *Hartford Courant archives*

Above left: Albert Pope first saw a bicycle at the Centennial Exposition in Philadelphia in 1876, and by the mid-1890s he was manufacturing a quarter-million bicycles a year in Hartford's Frog Hollow neighborhood. A few years later, he branched out into automobiles, but that success was short-lived. *Hartford Courant archives*

Above right: Men on high-wheel bicycles parade along Hartford's Main Street in the 1890s, in this photograph by Charles T. Stuart. The steeple is of Center Congregational Church. *The Connecticut Historical Society*

Right: A Pope-Hartford police patrol van. *The Connecticut Historical Society*

Above: Women quickly embraced the freedom and mobility the bicycle gave them, so much so that suffragist Susan B. Anthony declared, "The bicycle has done more for the emancipation of women than anything in the world." Members of the Hartford Ladies Cycle Club pause for a rest at the Soldiers and Sailors Memorial Arch in the 1890s.
Hartford Courant archives

THE RAIN OF PARKS

In the mid-1890s, Hartford was showered with what was called "the rain of parks." In a span of little more than a year — August 1894 to November 1895 — Pope, Elizabeth, Goodwin, Riverside and Keney parks came into existence, ringing the city.

"It should be the aim of the city not to have these parks mere isolated spots of ground for decorative purposes but a continuous property," an article in The Courant noted in December 1894, "for the benefit of all the people, especially for those people who are unable to enjoy the large grounds and gardens which those more fortunate have. They should be for the daily use of the people and no part of the city should be neglected in the movement."

Before the 1850s, the city had few open spaces except for a few small greens. The Rev. Horace Bushnell proposed the city's first park — to be laid out between the Park River and Trinity College, which later moved to make way for the new state Capitol — and Frederick Law Olmsted was asked to design it. Olmsted was busy with New York City's Central Park, so the city of Hartford hired his friend Jacob Weidenmann to design and build the park, which was completed in the early 1860s. Bushnell Park was the first municipal park — funded and approved by a vote of city residents — in the country.

Then in the 1890s, the Rev. Francis Goodwin, a wealthy amateur botanist and architect, persuaded some of the city's largest landowners to give their lands to the city for parks.

As the Rev. William De Loss Love Jr. said at the dedication of Elizabeth Park, "There is no other city in all our land which can produce a parallel of such timely and effective generosity in connection with its system of parks."

Above left: Boys in knickers and caps, some of them barefoot, climb poles and ropes, and girls in dresses and stockings swing around a maypole at the outdoor gymnasium at Pope Park in 1908. *The Connecticut Historical Society*

Above right: Schoolboys do calisthenics at Pope Park in 1914. *Hartford Courant archives*

Above: Formally dressed men and women gather for a picnic at Goodwin Park in the early 1900s. *The Connecticut Historical Society*

Above: Boys start to organize an ice hockey game as skaters move across the frozen Park River at Trumbull and Jewell streets in December 1892, in sight of the fire bell tower.
Hartford Courant archives

Above: The north side of Asylum Street between Ann and High streets in Hartford, circa 1895. *The Connecticut Historical Society*

Left: Gold Street in Hartford prior to being widened in 1899. *The Connecticut Historical Society*

Below: G. Fox department store on Main Street in Hartford. *Hartford Courant archives*

Right: Samuel Clemens (Mark Twain) and his wife, Livy Clemens, sit on the long porch or "ombra" of their home on Farmington Avenue in Hartford with their daughters, from left, Clara, Jean and Susy Clemens, and their dog Hash in 1885. *Mark Twain House and Museum*

Below: Mark Twain's house, circa 1874-1881. *Mark Twain House and Museum*

Above left: Pratt & Whitney Co.'s Small Tool Division, shown in 1911, was originally on Flower Street off Capitol Avenue in Hartford's Frog Hollow neighborhood.
The Connecticut Historical Society

Above top right: An engraving of the Weed Sewing Machine Co. on Capitol Avenue in about 1875. *The Connecticut Historical Society*

Above bottom right: Alfred C. Fuller started his brush company in a shed on Park Street in 1906 that he rented for $8 a month. Horse-drawn wagons delivered cartons of brushes, mops and brooms to local dealers who sold them door to door and to Union Station for shipment to dealers around the country. *Hartford Courant archives*

Above left: Brainard Field is dedicated on June 11, 1921. The first airmail planes to fly into Hartford originally landed in Goodwin Park, beginning in 1918. After a plane crashed in 1920, killing two airmen in front of people playing tennis and golf, Mayor Newton Brainard had a municipal airfield constructed in a 350-acre cow pasture in the South Meadows. When it was dedicated, Brainard Field was the only municipal airport between New York and Boston. The mayor, however, was on vacation, and did not attend the opening day air show. *The Connecticut Historical Society*

Above middle: Baxter's Painting and Decorating Store at 50 Church St., in a 1918 photograph by William G. Dudley. *The Connecticut Historical Society*

Above right: Hartford's first skyscraper was the Hartford National Bank Building on Main Street, across from the Old State House. Built in 1912 and later known as the Hartford-Aetna Building, it was demolished in 1990. The bank, shown in a postcard that was mailed in 1913, had its origins on the same block in 1792. *Tomas J. Nenortas Collection*

Right: Main Street in the late 1920s, looking north. The Old State House is at right. *Hartford Courant archives*

Above: Produce carts line Front Street on Hartford's East Side in about 1935, in front of shops including Brooklyn Market, London's Barber Shop and J.R. Loan Company. Some prices can be seen: 2 lbs. of butter for 53 cents, 10 lbs. of sugar for 51 cents and 2 dozen eggs for 53 cents. *Hartford History Center / Hartford Public Library*

Above: The Charter Oak Bridge opens on Sept. 5, 1942. The original 10-cent toll had increased to 35 cents by 1989, when tolls were eliminated on state highways and bridges. *Hartford Courant*

Above right: In 1996 the Old State House is surrounded by skyscrapers but still anchors downtown Hartford. *Michael Kodas / Hartford Courant*

Right: "Quenticut," a sculpture created in 2001 by Clyde Lynds, stands at the entryway of Riverfront Plaza in Hartford. The name is derived from the Algonquin word for long tidal river. *Michael McAndrews / Hartford Courant*

Above: A Hartford man fishes at Charter Oak Landing in October 2012.
Michael McAndrews / Hartford Courant

Left: The Connecticut Science Center, designed by architect Cesar Pelli and opened in May 2009, is aglow at night and reflected in the Connecticut River. The iconic Travelers Tower is in the background. *Stephen Dunn / Hartford Courant*

OUR
CHANGING SCENERY

Connecticut is a small state but it packs a lot of landscape into its 5,543 square miles. A glacier pushing its way to Long Island Sound littered the land with stones that early farmers piled into the state's distinctive stone walls.

Early settlers also felled Connecticut's forests to create farms, but much of the forest has grown back in the past century. Even so, in 2012, Connecticut clocked a 22 percent increase in the number of farms in just five years, to nearly 6,000.

The state boasts more than 1,000 lakes and ponds and 8,400 miles of rivers and streams.

Nearly 100 rivers in Connecticut drain into the Sound, a rich mix of fresh and salt water that is home to more than 1,200 invertebrate species and 170 species of fish. Connecticut's 271 miles of shoreline are rippled with 16 harbors, and shores and marshes are crucial stopping points for tens of thousands of migrating birds.

In recent decades, as billions have been spent to improve sewage treatment plants and curb pollution, once-threatened eagles and ospreys have returned to nest along the Sound and the rivers that feed into it.

The built landscape has evolved as well. Connecticut is the fourth most densely populated state, with nearly 3.6 million people living in nearly 1.5 million housing units. The state's architectural heritage is a dynamic mix of old and new — from the simple saltbox houses of the 17th century's Puritans and the Georgian Colonials of the 18th century's more prosperous merchants to the intricate confections of the High Victorian style and the 20th century's Arts and Crafts, Modernist and Urban Modern movements.

Left: The Washburn Preserve in Branford offers views from the marshy banks of Long Island Sound to the Thimble Islands. *Patrick Raycraft / Hartford Courant*

Above: Swimmers and boaters enjoy Swan Beach on Long Island Sound in Old Lyme in the early 1900s.
The Connecticut Historical Society

Opposite left: The Housatonic River flows over a dam in Derby, below a now unused gatehouse. In the 17th century, European colonists dammed smaller streams to power mills, and by the late 18th century, dams began to appear on larger rivers. The state estimates that at least 4,000 dams remain in Connecticut on its approximately 6,000 miles of streams. *Michael McAndrews / Hartford Courant*

Opposite right: Devin "Moe" Booth of Thomaston, a fishing guide and instructor, casts his fly rod in the Farmington River near the Town Bridge in Collinsville in August 2004. The increase in population, dams, farming and industry in the state over the decades put a lot of stress on rivers that wasn't reversed until the environmental movements of the 1960s. *Stephen Dunn / Hartford Courant*

RIVERS RUN THROUGH IT

Connecticut's waterways are a significant and usually appealing aspect of the landscape, but, with rare exception, they are radically different from the pristine wilds of four centuries ago.

Since the 17th century, hundreds of brooks, streams and rivers have been dammed, sometimes wiping out entire strains of migratory fish like salmon and shad, and fundamentally altering the ecology of long stretches of river.

The state's waterways were severely degraded by industrial and sewage pollution. Many were further harmed by invasive plant or animal species. With native fish populations greatly reduced, exotic species were introduced, usually intentionally. Parts of some rivers, like the Park River in Hartford, were deemed so polluted or flood-prone that they were entombed in culverts, covered over and paved.

Connecticut was among the earliest states to seriously tackle water pollution, creating its own Clean Water Act in 1967 and beginning work to either upgrade antiquated wastewater treatment plants or build new ones where none existed. Industry was told to treat its wastes before discharging them into a river.

By the early 1970s, with the new water pollution standards well along, water quality in the rivers began to improve. Within 15 years, there was dramatic improvement in water quality in many rivers throughout the state.

Suddenly, there was a resurgence of recreation on rivers, many of them once badly polluted.

But the easiest water quality improvements have been made, and many of the state's rivers, although greatly improved, are not as clean as they could be.

A LAND BORN TO BE WILD

The Connecticut forest 400 years ago was a rich mix of species, often park-like, without much brush in the understory. In places, native Americans burned patches of forest to keep them open, but much of the state was simply mature, pristine forest.

By the time The Connecticut Courant began publication in 1764, the population in the colonies had grown substantially, which led to a rapid loss of forest cover. For roughly the next 80 years, the percentage of the state in forest would plummet.

On April 22, 1817, The Courant published a column by the lexicographer Noah Webster titled "Domestic Economy." It was a reaction to deforestation and one of the first pleas for conservation in the U.S.

Noting that the state already was extensively cleared, Webster argued that it could no longer sustain the enormous amount of wood burned each year in homes. It was time for efficiencies and a conservation ethic.

"But we are not merely to seek the means of subsistence for ourselves — we are not to waste and destroy, for the sake of present enjoyment; we must not strip the inheritance of its wood & its fences and its timber, and leave it barren and impoverished for the next generation," Webster wrote. "We must not be so improvident as to render our country uninhabitable."

Around 1850, only about 30 percent of Connecticut was forested, and even then the trees were often young and small.

By 1970, nearly 70 percent of Connecticut was forested, with many of the trees sizable and at or near maturity. It happened slowly over more than a century, but the transformation of the landscape was dramatic.

Above left: A brook winds through Meshomasic State Forest in Portland, the first state forest in Connecticut and New England, and the second in the country. The state originally acquired 70 acres of forest for $105 in 1903, to demonstrate good forest management practices for private landowners. The state forest now spans about 9,000 acres, primarily in Portland, East Hampton and Marlborough, with smaller sections in Glastonbury and Hebron.
Bob MacDonnell / Hartford Courant

Above middle: Rebecca Bishop rides a horse amid vibrant fall foliage at Folly Farm at the base of Talcott Mountain in Simsbury in 2005.
Tom Brown / Hartford Courant

Above right: The Nathan Hale Homestead in Coventry was built in 1777 and added to the National Register of Historic Places in 1970. *Hartford Courant file photo*

Above: The Hartford skyline is visible from Wickham Park in Manchester beyond woods aflame in fall colors during the Central Connecticut Conference cross country championships in October 2013. *John Woike / Hartford Courant*

Right: Haley Fox Billipp and Andy Billipp farm the historic 60-acre Eddy Farm in the center of Newington, farmed by Haley's family for generations. *Stephen Dunn / Hartford Courant*

Below left: Shareholders pick up produce from the Shundahi Farm in Mansfield in August 2012. *Mark Mirko / Hartford Courant*

Below middle: Jorge Cardoso thins peach blossoms at Rogers Orchards in Southington in May 2014 for harvest in mid-summer. *John Woike / Hartford Courant*

Below right: Field workers Juan Torres, left, and Hugo Flores harvest pumpkins at Cohen Farms in Ellington in September 2006. *Bob MacDonnell / Hartford Courant*

Opposite: Geese at Bogue Farms in Higganum are fattened for the holidays in 2007. *John Woike / Hartford Courant*

MAKING 'MODERN' HISTORY

One of the most remarkable periods in the history of Connecticut's evolving architectural landscape was from the late 1940s to the late 1960s, when a group of Harvard-trained architects took up residence in the town of New Canaan and made modern history.

Known as "The Harvard Five," Eliot Noyes, Philip Johnson, Landis Gores, John Johansen and their teacher Marcel Breuer built homes for themselves and others that were nothing like the traditional clapboard Colonials with pitched roofs and many-paned windows that dotted the leafy town.

These architects took a gutsy new approach in their Mid-Century Modern designs, using broad horizontal lines, exposed steel beams, dramatic cantilevers, spare detailing and massive walls of glass that blurred the line between the inside and the great outdoors.

Above: The most famous of the Mid-Century Modern houses in New Canaan is the see-through Glass House, which Philip Johnson designed in 1949 and lived in until his death in 2005.
Michael McAndrews / Hartford Courant

Above: The Jacob Strong Homestead is one of the oldest buildings in Torrington.
Richard Messina / Hartford Courant

Left: Hartford's signature "Perfect Sixes" on Park Terrace.
Christine Palm / Special to The Courant

Above: A juxtaposition of architectural styles in Hartford: The Phoenix Company's famed two-sided "Boat Building" and the Travelers Tower, the seventh-tallest building in the world when it was built in 1919. *Michael McAndrews / Hartford Courant*

AN EMBLEM OF THE GILDED AGE

Designed and constructed at the height of Hartford's Gilded Age, the Connecticut Capitol is an opulent emblem of the city's wealth, from the burnished walnut paneling in the House chamber to the detailed engraving on the brass door hinges.

Architect Richard M. Upjohn made his name designing churches, and the Capitol bears traces of his earlier work. The stained glass is an obvious similarity, as are the water fountains, which resemble baptismal fonts.

The fountains are purely decorative now, but when the building opened, they were used to fill buckets to provide water for legislators' horses.

James Batterson, a powerful Hartford businessman who founded The Travelers, wanted to be involved in the construction of the new Capitol. He submitted plans with George Keller, the designer of the Soldiers and Sailors Memorial Arch in Bushnell Park, but lost the commission to Upjohn.

But Batterson still kept his hands in things by becoming the superintendent of the project, which allowed him to tinker with Upjohn's design. The building's distinct architecture, high-Victorian Gothic, with Italianate and classical elements, is the legacy of the artistic tension between the two men.

One of the elements that Upjohn originally envisioned was a clock tower at the top of the building. But Batterson and others on the committee overseeing the construction wanted a dome, which they believed would give the Capitol a greater sense of authority.

Right: Fireworks over the state Capitol kick off the official celebration of Connecticut's 350th birthday in January 1985. *Steve Silk / Hartford Courant*

Above: The graceful double arches of the Arrigoni Bridge over the Connecticut River, with the city of Middletown beyond.

Patrick Raycraft / Hartford Courant

THE PLACES WE CALL HOME

D ig into the history of Connecticut's 169 towns and cities and you'll find that each one is distinctive, with its own idiosyncracies and claims to fame.

The first machine-made nuts and bolts were made in Southington. The first silk mill in the U.S. was built in Mansfield.

The Scoville Memorial Library in Salisbury, which was founded in 1771 as the Smith Library, was the first publicly funded library in the country.

In 2002 the Coca-Cola Co. debuted Vanilla Coke at The Vanilla Bean Cafe in Pomfret.

The first copper coins in the Colonies were minted in 1737 in Simsbury by Samuel Higley, who used ore from his Copper Hill Mine; the mine later became Old Newgate Prison.

The Subway restaurants and Schick shaving products companies are both headquartered in Milford.

Albert Einstein had a summer home in Old Lyme.

The board game Scrabble was named and developed in Newtown.

Brooklyn hosts the country's oldest continually operating agricultural fair.

The Pez candy company's factory and museum are in Orange.

Artificial snow-making got its start in Cornwall, at the Mohawk Mountain Ski Area, in 1950.

The Courant's coverage of Connecticut's cities and towns, large and small, for 250 years has often highlighted the distinctions that set them apart.

But the places we call home, from Andover to Woodstock, have much in common, and we celebrate these shared experiences as well: parades and road races, families gathering for holidays, shoppers looking for bargains, the daily rhythms of work and play.

Left: In an Avon classroom in 1911, heat came from a Franklin stove. Students are memorizing lessons on the blackboard and learning that the Rev. Thomas Hooker founded Hartford.
Hartford Courant archives

Above left: Girls age 8, 9 and 10 string tobacco in the shed at Hawthorn Farm in the Hazardville section of Enfield. *Lewis Hine / Library of Congress*

Above right: A truckload of workers, many of them children, gather at Post Office Square in Hartford at 6 a.m. on Aug. 7, 1917, to head for the American Sumatra tobacco farm in South Windsor. *Lewis Hine / Library of Congress*

Right: Three "leaf boys," age 9, 9 and 11, at the Cybalski tobacco farm in the Hazardville section of Enfield in 1917. *Lewis Hine / Library of Congress*

Above: The state had been issuing license plates for only about 20 years when this car — with a plate that reads "T-7, CONN 1928" — was on the road. *Hartford Courant archives*

Above right: A moving company van in New Haven in 1902, photographed by T.S. Bronson. *Hartford Courant archives*

Below right: When Theodore Roosevelt visited Hartford in 1902, he became the first American president to ride in an automobile, and it was an automobile manufactured by Albert Pope in Hartford, as were the bicycles that surrounded the car. *The Connecticut Historical Society*

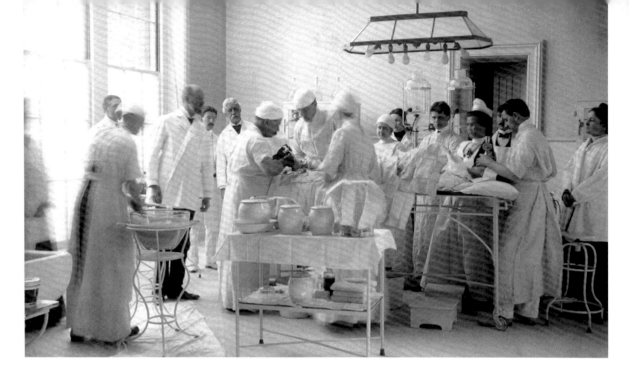

Right: Doctors and nurses do not yet wear masks or gloves in this operating room in Hartford Hospital, photographed circa 1900, which was situated to make use of sunlight pouring in the windows. The hospital was wired for electric lights in 1899.
T. Stewart Hamilton Archives / Hartford Hospital

Below: The original St. Francis Hospital building at the corner of Collins and Woodland streets in Hartford was an abandoned three-story brick house owned by Bishop Michael Tierney, photographed circa 1897.
St. Francis Hospital and Medical Center

Opposite top: The Women's League, founded in 1917 to meet the needs of migrant and immigrant families in Hartford, offered child care for working families and single mothers entering the work force. This photo dates from the 1930s. *Women's League Child Development Center*

Opposite below left: Children head to Camp Courant in 1939. *Hartford Courant archives*

Opposite below right: Children take part in an oral hygiene exercise at South Manchester Open-Air School in the early 1920s. Open-air schools aimed to promote better health, particularly for children predisposed to tuberculosis. *The Connecticut Historical Society*

Opposite top: Young mothers stroll with baby carriages in Windsor Locks in 1954. *Hartford Courant archives*

Opposite bottom left: Shoppers crowd the sidewalks in July 1954 as merchants at more than 70 stores in West Hartford Center and at Bishops Corner team up to hold sales for West Hartford Days. *Arthur Warmsley / Hartford Courant*

Opposite bottom right: At the Windsor Locks Centennial Parade on May 30, 1954, Centennial Queen Jane Pastomerlo rides with her attendants, from left, Nancy Fuller and Lorraine Weatherbee. *Art J. Kiely Jr. / Hartford Courant*

Top left: New York sirloin steaks sell for 75 cents a pound, T-bones for 85 cents a pound, and bananas for 11 cents a pound at the Stop & Shop at Bristol Plaza in 1960. *Arman G. Hatsian / Hartford Courant*

Bottom left: Members of Brownie Troop 61 from Hartford's Burns Elementary School carry a banner along rain-soaked Farmington Avenue during the 1979 Memorial Day parade. *Mary Alice Dwyer / Hartford Courant*

Below: Sportsmen make a splash in the log-rolling contest at the nine-day Connecticut Sportsmen's and Boat Show, held at the State Armory in Hartford in January 1953. *Hartford Courant archives*

Left: Members of the East Lyme High School Viking Marching Band parade in front of the state Capitol in January 1985.
Steve Silk / Hartford Courant

Below left: Visitors ride on the Bushnell Park carousel in April 1977.
Michael McAndrews / Hartford Courant

Below right: Teachers take a head count of kindergarten students at M.D. Fox School in February 1982. *Hartford Courant file photo*

Opposite: From left, George Hardy, Donald Griffin Jr., Christine Griffin and Lucille Hanna of Main Street in Hebron watch a parade go by in 1982.
Kathy Hanley / Hartford Courant

Above: Debbie Vincent of Middletown, in hat, sells cosmetics on the first floor of the G. Fox & Co. store in Hartford in 1983. The 11-story G. Fox building was constructed in 1918 and closed as a retail outlet in 1993. It now houses Capital Community College. *John Long / Hartford Courant*

Left: Roller skaters take advantage of the sloping state Capitol grounds and a warm day in March 1981. *Tony Bacewicz / Hartford Courant*

Opposite: Audrey M. Crandall, the clerk who ran the Windsorville Post Office in East Windsor, finishes paperwork to close the tiny station in November 1983. *Tony Bacewicz / Hartford Courant*

Opposite top left: Matt Roark, a second-grader at Gilead Hill School in Hebron, leans in for a closer look at a turkey at the Hebron Harvest Fair in September 1996, joined by classmates including Billy Zysk, center, and Chris Bray, right. *Kathy Hanley / Hartford Courant*

Opposite bottom left: Donald Grant cleans the stalls in a barn at his family's dairy farm in East Windsor early on a rainy morning in October 1985. *Dan Haar / Hartford Courant*

Opposite right: Sister Rose, right, of St. Joseph's Residence keeps an eye on Skipper, one of the pets at the home for the elderly, in October 1983 as resident Kathleen MacArthur checks the program for a blessing of animals. *John Long / Hartford Courant*

Above: Runners compete in the Manchester Road Race on Thanksgiving in 1977. The annual race started with 12 runners in 1927. It was canceled for a decade during the Depression and resumed in 1945. *John Long / Hartford Courant*

Opposite top: Olinda Seguro of Newington carries a flag as members of the Portugese folk-dancing group Rancho Folclarico de Hartford assemble during groundbreaking ceremonies in November 1983 for the new Our Lady of Fatima Church building on Madison Avenue in Hartford. *Tony Bacewicz / Hartford Courant*

Opposite bottom left: Simon Rozinsky, left, and Samuel Goldman lead the Torah procession of 26 men at the start of ceremonies dedicating Beth Sholom Synagogue on Cornwall Street in Hartford in November 1957. *Arthur Warmsley / Hartford Courant*

Opposite bottom right: Hundreds gather at Metropolitan A.M.E. Zion Church in Hartford for an Easter vigil in 1971. *Al Ferreira / Hartford Courant*

Above: The Nowobilski family of New Britain — including grandsons Bill and Mike Misko, their mother Barbara Misko and her parents Harry and Stasia Nowobilski — stand before a table set with a traditional Easter meal of lamb, smoked Polish sausage, eggs, breads and pastries in 1985. *Dennis Yonan / Hartford Courant*

Top right: Tracy Hellwig, 8; Carli Cayne, 7, and Lee Harder, 7, sing Christmas carols in front of the Eno Memorial Hall in Simsbury in 1980. *Kirk Hatsian / Hartford Courant*

Middle right: After attending Easter Mass in 1987 at the Immaculate Conception Church on Park Street in Hartford, Nidia Fuentes, 5, left; Yadira Vazquez, 4; and Yadira's brother Juan, 6, sit outside the church to eat Easter sundaes. *Shana Sureck / Hartford Courant*

Bottom right: Jose Baez, a town parks department worker, installs holiday decorations over Main Street in downtown East Hartford in 1992. *Dan Haar / Hartford Courant*

Left: Kendrick Diaz, 4, of East Hartford, a student at the American School for the Deaf in West Hartford, meets Santa at Westfarms Mall's first-ever "Signing Santa Day" in December 2012. Students were invited to sign with Santa, have their faces painted and play games at the event. *Richard Messina / Hartford Courant*

Above: Jerome Taylor, 11, of South Windsor, negotiates with a reluctant participant in a "Living Creche" at the Bloomfield United Methodist Church in December 1990. *Bob Stern / Special to The Courant*

Opposite: Rabbi Mendel Samuels, center, prepares to read from the Torah during a Purim service at the Chabad House of the Valley in Simsbury in March 2005. Helping the rabbi are, from left, Bruce Friedland of Simsbury; Rabbi Moshe Smith, who is Rabbi Samuels' father-in-law; and Rick Blum of Burlington. *Stephen Dunn / Hartford Courant*

Above: Best man Chevon Schand, 17, lays down a decorative broom for bride Betty Lynn Lauray, 20, and his brother, groom Shamel Lateek Schand, 23, for the "Jumping of the Broom" ritual at a wedding ceremony at Shiloh Baptist Church on Albany Avenue in Hartford in May 2004. *Patrick Raycraft / Hartford Courant*

Above: Paul Jones and Myra Jones, wearing the same dress she wore on their wedding day in 1942, renew their wedding vows at River Ridge, a senior living community in Avon, on Valentine's Day in 2008. *Rick Hartford / Hartford Courant*

Top right: Blanca Hernandez, left, sews custom-made soccer nets at the InCord factory in Colchester in 2011. *Stephen Dunn / Hartford Courant*

Bottom right: Adrian Stock builds a custom bike wheel in Guilford in 2007. *Michael Kodas / Hartford Courant*

Opposite: Mackenzie Frazer, 7, waits to perform with his band class during the Green Street Arts Center's Winter Solstice Celebration in Middletown in December 2009. *Bettina Hansen / Hartford Courant*

Below: Executive chef Scott Miller puts the finishing touch on a dish of Connecticut shad and roe at Max's Oyster Bar in West Hartford in April 2012. *Patrick Raycraft / Hartford Courant*

Above left: Hartford Symphony Orchestra Conductor Carolyn Kuan leads students from the Expeditionary Learning Academy at Moylan School in Hartford in a performance of "Ode to Joy" during the symphony's Annual Gala at the Club at Rentschler Field in East Hartford in September 2012.
David Butler II / Special to The Courant

Above middle: Dancers perform at the Riverfront Dragon Boat and Asian Festival at Mortensen Riverfront Plaza in August 2012.
Brad Horrigan / Hartford Courant

Above right: Fiesta del Norte band members, from left, Margarito Mello, Dave Giardina and Larry Gareau perform mariachi music outside the Charter Oak Cultural Center in Hartford during the center's Putting Down Roots children's organic gardening program in July 2012.
Mark Mirko / Hartford Courant

Left: Dancers with the Nutmeg Balleg's "Nutcracker 2005" wait backstage at The Bushnell. *John Long / Hartford Courant*

Opposite: Erick Inhphom, left, performs a breakdancing routine while John Bendezu also practices at Real Art Ways in January 2009. The art installation by Carol Padberg is called "Face Value."
Ross Taylor / Hartford Courant

Above: Berlin High School teacher David Bosso, center, works with students, from left, Brandon Rocco, Kayla Cervoni, Olivia Martino and Ally Schulz. Bosso was the 2012 Connecticut Teacher of the Year. *Mark Mirko / Hartford Courant*

Left: Olayinka Edwards, center, hugs her classmate Nafissa Salihou before lining up to enter the First Cathedral in Bloomfield for the Windsor High School graduation ceremony in June 2007. *Stephen Dunn / Hartford Courant*

Opposite: In the front row, Alexander Farrah, 11, and his brother Spencer Farrah, 13, and their grandparents, Cathie and Dr. Robert Jeresaty, wear special glasses to watch the premiere screening of the 3D movie "Dinosaurs Alive" with others at the Connecticut Science Center in June 2009, a week before the center officially opened. *Stephen Dunn / Hartford Courant*

ANSWERING THE CALL

When the first shots were fired at Lexington and Concord in April 1775, Connecticut quickly rallied 3,700 men to fight in six regiments of the newly formed Continental Army under George Washington.

In the American Revolution, Connecticut would produce one of the war's greatest heroes, Nathan Hale, hanged as a spy at age 21, and its worst traitor, Benedict Arnold, a decorated soldier for the Colonies who then switched allegiance to the British and commanded the forces that burned New London and Groton.

Gov. Jonathan Trumbull was the only royal governor in the Colonies who supported the American cause, and he pledged the state's resources in the fight for independence from Great Britain.

Connecticut supplied the Continental Army with more food and cannons than any other state. The state's wool, cotton, silk and thread industries helped produce cloth for blankets and uniforms.

While war raged in surrounding colonies, Connecticut enjoyed relative peace. The manufacturers and farmers continued to churn out goods, foodstuffs and livestock, sending

Left: These eight soldiers from Connecticut's 26th Regiment served at the Siege of Port Hudson, Louisiana, during the Civil War in 1863. The regiment lost nearly 20 percent of its men.
Middlesex County Museum and Historical Society

arms, tents, food, clothing, gunpowder and cannonballs to the U.S. troops. Dubbed the "Provision State," Connecticut also supplied raw materials — iron, saltpeter to make gunpowder, salt to preserve food.

And about 30,000 men served in the war.

It wouldn't be the last time that Connecticut's people would head into conflicts that shaped the American experience, many laying down their lives to defend cherished beliefs and safeguard liberty.

During the Civil War, 53,721 men served in Connecticut regiments; there were 20,000 casualties, including 4,891 deaths and 400 men missing.

The Provision State again played a key role in military supply in that war. The output of the great 19th- and 20th-century gunmakers of the Connecticut River Valley from Springfield to New Haven earned the region another nickname — "The Arsenal of Democracy." The Colt Armory alone manufactured 387,017 revolvers, 6,693 rifles and 113,980 muskets for the Civil War. Sharps in Hartford produced 30,000 rifles a year. Remington Arms of Bridgeport made half of the Army's small arms cartridges. Winchester Arms in New Haven manufactured 16,000 Browning automatic rifles.

Connecticut's heritage of defense innovations extends far beyond firearms. From Salisbury to Bridgeport to Groton, the far corners of the state developed iron forging, launched ships and submarines, and advanced aerospace.

Into the 20th and 21st centuries, Connecticut answered the call. The state sent 66,855 into the battlefields of World War I. During World War II, 220,000 men and women served; 4,357 died, another 400 were left missing. In the Korean War, 326 Connecticut military personnel lost their lives. The war in Vietnam claimed 612.

The technology of modern warfare has meant fewer deaths among Connecticut's military — seven in the Gulf War, 51 in Iraq and Afghanistan — but has resulted in new hazards. Lingering symptoms of uncertain origin came to be recognized as Gulf War Syndrome, after persistent campaigning by those affected, including Maj. Michael Donnelly of South Windsor.

Later in Iraq and Afghanistan, soldiers started coming home with savage wounds and multiple amputations — injuries that would have killed them in earlier wars. Improving medical technology meant more soldiers were surviving, but at a high cost.

And the profound and lasting psychological damage the traumatic stress of war can cause — an issue The Courant wrote about as far back as 1921 — emerged as a more common scourge for returning veterans.

A FORTUNE SPENT, A REPUTATION RUINED

Wethersfield merchant Silas Deane played a central role arranging for shiploads of supplies and enlisting European officers, including the Marquis de Lafayette and Baron von Steuben, for George Washington's army. The goods Deane secured were crucial to the Americans' victory at Saratoga, an early turning point in the war; without that pivotal victory it was unlikely France would have openly backed the Americans in their fight against British rule.

But Deane also was accused of wartime profiteering. He was vilified toward the end of his life nearly as much as traitor Benedict Arnold, left financially destitute and quite possibly poisoned by his former pupil and secretary who, it turns out, was a British double agent.

It wasn't until 50 years after his death that Congress cleared his name and reimbursed to his family some of the vast personal fortune Deane spent to help the Americans win independence.

Right: Painting of Silas Deane by William Johnson, 1766. *Webb-Deane-Stevens Museum*

ABOARD THE ONE-MAN 'TURTLE'

S gt. Ezra Lee of Lyme piloted the first combat submarine during the early days of the American Revolution, wedging his body into a one-man contraption that plunged into New York Harbor with the goal of blowing up a British warship.

Designed as an attack vessel in the early 1770s by Yale College student David Bushnell, the "Turtle" resembled two joined half-barrels, with enough room inside for one person. Its exterior was equipped with a large screw that could be twisted into the planks of a ship's hull.

The screw was tethered by a rope to an oaken keg with 150 pounds of gunpowder and a timing device fashioned with the assistance of a clock maker.

Lee's gutsy attempted sabotage of British Admiral Lord Richard Howe's flagship "Eagle" did not succeed, and later missions were beset by navigational problems and tides.

East Lyme Historical Society and Submarine Force Library and Museum

Above: Israel Putnam was a farmer in Colonial Connecticut, living on land near what is now Pomfret. He proved his courage in the French and Indian War and became a legend for his exploits at Bunker Hill early in the American Revolution.
"Putnam Leaving The Plow," by Kellogg & Bulkeley, 1886 / The Connecticut Historical Society

Left: Three Connecticut soldiers — Daniel Bissell, Daniel Brown and Elijah Churchill — were the first recipients of a military honor for their heroic feats during the Revolutionary War: mounting daring raids behind British lines, facing enemy fire in combat and infiltrating the British army as a spy. George Washington instituted the award in 1782 as the Badge of Military Merit, and it later became the most well-known honor in the U.S. military: the Purple Heart. This painting by H. Charles McBarron depicts the ceremony at which Churchill and Brown received the honor.
U.S. Army Center of Military History

BATTLE OF GETTYSBURG, PA. JULY 3⁰ 1863.

PRISONERS OF WAR

By August 1864, the infamous Confederate war camp at Andersonville, Georgia, intended for only 10,000 captives, held more than 33,000 Union prisoners in a space roughly half the size of Bushnell Park.

Conditions were filthy, disease was rampant, and soldiers also died from malnutrition and exposure to the elements. More than 300 of the 13,000 who died at Andersonville were from Connecticut.

Pvt. Dorence Atwater of Terryville, who was among the first prisoners there, assisted the camp surgeon in logging camp deaths, and at great risk to himself he secretly kept his own copy of the death registry.

After the war, Atwater and Clara Barton, who later founded the American Red Cross, were able to mark the graves of many whose gravesites otherwise would have been unknown. Today Andersonville is the site of the National Prisoner of War Museum, honoring POWs from all the nation's wars.

Right: Prisoners endured ghastly conditions and thousands died at the infamous Confederate war camp in Andersonville, Ga. *Essex Library*

Above: Tapped by President Lincoln, Glastonbury native and newspaper editor Gideon Welles served as secretary of the Navy from 1861 to 1869. During the Civil War, he planned and oversaw the blockade of Southern ports along 3,500 miles of coastline. *The Connecticut Historical Society*

Below left: Wethersfield members of the 22nd Connecticut Volunteers take their ease in camp after enlisting in August 1862. *Wethersfield Historical Society*

Opposite: Connecticut soldiers participated in the major Civil War Battle of Gettysburg, portrayed in this lithograph by E.B. and E.C. Kellogg of Hartford. The Kellogg brothers ran a local printing company that published thousands of images of local scenes and historic moments. They likely got verbal accounts of Civil War battles via telegram. *The Connecticut Historical Society*

Above: Douglass Fowler of Norwalk had already served two tours as a Union soldier when he took command of the 17th Connecticut Volunteer Infantry. On July 1, 1863, he was among the first to head into battle at Gettysburg, Pa. Astride a white horse, Fowler joked about the artillery rounds whizzing past, telling his soldiers, "Dodge the big ones, boys!" But one of those cannon shots slammed into his head. His fearlessness made him a legend. *Bobby Dobbins Collection / seventeenthcvi.org*

Right: Arthur J. Kiely Jr. left his job as a Hartford Courant photographer in 1943 to join the Marines. He became a combat photographer and spent the rest of World War II documenting the devastation. This 1944 photo is from his album, "Battle of the Marianas," covering the World War II battles of Saipan, Tinian and Guam. Kiely was awarded the Bronze Star for gallantry in combat in Saipan. After the war, Kiely returned to The Courant newsroom, later moving on to Pratt & Whitney and then the Connecticut Historical Society, to which he donated many of his war images.

Art Kiely Jr. / The Connecticut Historical Society

Opposite: James Stanizzi, 18, embraces his mother, Jennie Stanizzi, and holds the hand of Frances, his wife of two months, just before departing on a train with the 43rd Division for Camp Pickett, Va., in 1950 during the Korean War.

Harry Batz / Hartford Courant

SAVING OTHERS FROM CERTAIN DEATH

Air Force Sgt. John Lee Levitow of Glastonbury, winner of the Medal of Honor, salutes the bullet-torn American flag he raised at a ceremony in Newington on May 29, 1970.

The Defense Department said Levitow saved his fellow crew members from certain death one February night in 1969. He was on an AC-47 fixed-wing gunship, flying low over the jungles of Vietnam, dropping flares to illuminate the night for soldiers fighting on the ground, when the plane was struck by a mortar round. The explosion ripped a 2-foot hole through a wing and also knocked an activated flare from a crew member's grasp.

The aircraft was partially out of control and the flare was rolling around wildly inside the plane. Despite a concussion and 40 shrapnel wounds in his back and legs, Levitow threw himself on the smoking flare, dragged himself to the rear of the plane and pushed the flare through the open cargo door. It ignited in the air — but clear of the aircraft.

Above: Arman G. Hatsian / Hartford Courant

Above: About 1,000 antiwar demonstrators march down State Street on May 13, 1972, on their way to I-91 where they blocked southbound traffic for 20 minutes. Later, the demonstrators, most of them college-age students, raised a Viet Cong flag in front of the Federal Building on Main Street. *Harry Batz / Hartford Courant*

Above: Moments after a mortar attack at the CMOC base in Fallujah, Iraq, hit a fuel pod in June 2006 and created a large blaze, Sgt. Terry Rathbun, right, of East Lyme and Capt. Harry Thompson of Las Vegas survey the damage. The mortars fired at the Charlie Company base also damaged equipment in the compound, but nobody was injured. *Tom Brown / Hartford Courant*

Opposite: Jesrene Daniel of Prospect hugs her son, David Tross, as he steps off the bus at the Connecticut State Armory on May 19, 2010, arriving home after a one-year deployment in Iraq. About 120 soldiers from the 192nd Military Police Battalion of Niantic returned to a jubilant crowd of friends and family. *Stephen Dunn / Hartford Courant*

THE CONSTITUTION STATE

Connecticut's love of politics dates back to 1639, when the freemen of Hartford, Wethersfield and Windsor adopted the Fundamental Orders of Connecticut, regarded as the first written democratic constitution establishing a representative government — hence "The Constitution State."

By 1662, John Winthrop Jr. obtained a royal charter for Connecticut. Legend has it that in 1687, when Britain sought to revoke the charter and incorporate Connecticut into the Dominion of New England, under direct control of a council appointed by the Crown, Colonists hid the charter in the hollow of a huge white oak tree in Hartford rather than surrender it to a British official. Despite defying royal authority, Connecticut continued to govern itself.

The state has witnessed many other historic political moments: Barack Obama's stirring XL Center speech on the cusp of a crucial primary

win; Ella Grasso's walk through the snow to the storm center after the Blizzard of 1978; Theodore Roosevelt becoming the first U.S. president to ride in an automobile when he visited Hartford; John F. Kennedy's speech on the steps of the Hartford Times on the eve of his presidential election.

But Connecticut's political history is also blemished by moments such as Gov. William T. Minor's resounding election in 1855 on a platform of unabashedly bigoted anti-Irish, anti-Catholic measures backed by the Know-Nothing movement. Not to mention the slew of corruption investigations and criminal convictions of political leaders, including Gov. John G. Rowland, state Treasurer Paul Silvester, Bridgeport Mayor Joseph Ganim, Waterbury Mayor Joseph Santopietro, Waterbury Mayor T. Frank Hayes and many other state and municipal officials.

While the rough and tumble of political debate and deal-making has long been a fascinating spectator sport, the state's political spirit isn't limited to passively observing political leaders in action.

In Connecticut, politics is also a participatory sport, and it doesn't take much to get activists and advocates riled up, out in public making their views known, pro and con, and pushing for change.

Left: Gov. M. Jodi Rell presents her budget address to House and Senate legislators in the Hall of the House at the state Capitol on Feb. 3, 2010.
Michael McAndrews / Hartford Courant

A NEW NATION PROCLAIMED; A HISTORIC LOSS

The Courant published the 1,137-word Declaration of Independence in elegant 8-point type at the bottom of Page 2 on July 15, 1776, under the heading, "Philadelphia, In Congress, July 4, 1776." John Hancock, president of the Continental Congress, is the only signer mentioned, but without his famous looping calligraphy. The author, Thomas Jefferson, is not named.

The momentous proclamation had to compete for readers' attention with a local scandal. Among the items on the back page of the four-page newspaper is a notice of "infidelity" on the part of Rebecca Carrington, wife of Salmon Carrington of Milford. There are also advertisements offering a $5 reward for deserters (a common problem during the Revolution, with the long lulls between battles) and runaway slave notices.

Although the declaration ran on Page 2, it was immensely important to Ebenezer Watson, publisher and printer of the Connecticut Courant and Weekly Intelligencer. Publishers like Watson, in the words of a contemporary, helped "spread the notice of the tyrannical Designs formed against America, and kindled a Spirit that has been sufficient to repel them."

Above right: For its April 15, 1865, edition, The Hartford Daily Courant hurried to add an Extra in its right-side eighth and ninth columns, on the news of the assassination of President Lincoln, headlined "Awful Calamity. Terrible Loss to the Nation!" The headline word ASSASSINATED! is crooked, as though the typesetter's hands had trembled with grief.

Right: On March 4, 1889, The Hartford Courant published a special supplement issued as a souvenir of the inauguration of President Harrison, headlined "Century of Presidents." The photograph of the U.S. Capitol on the cover was the first photograph The Courant published.

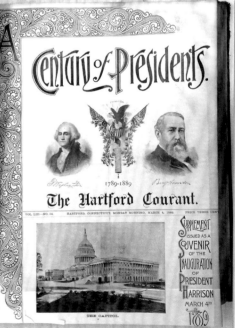

The Crowbar Governor

Morgan Bulkeley, who was vice president of Aetna Life Insurance Co. from 1879 until his death in 1922, devoted much of his time to political life and working to improve the city of Hartford.

In 1874 he founded the Hartford Dark Blues baseball team, the city's first professional sports franchise. Two years later, the Dark Blues became a charter member of the newly formed National League, with Bulkeley serving as the league's first president.

From 1880 to 1888, Bulkeley served as Hartford's mayor. He left city hall to serve a term as governor. When the legislature deadlocked over a successor, Bulkeley broke into his office and served a second term, earning him the nickname "The Crowbar Governor."

In the early 1900s, he played important roles in building the graceful stone bridge that bears his name, restoring the Old State House and erecting the state Supreme Court building. He also represented Connecticut in the U.S. Senate from 1905 to 1911.

Above left: Morgan Bulkeley. *Hartford Courant archives*

Above right: President Franklin Delano Roosevelt stopped in Hartford on Nov. 4 during his 1944 campaign tour. *Hartford Courant archives*

Right: President Harry S. Truman smiles as he signs his initials to the keel plate of the USS Nautilus, the world's first atomic-powered submarine, during a ceremony in Groton on June 14, 1952. Behind the president are, from left, John Jay Hopkins, president of General Dynamics Corp.; O.P. Robinson, general manager of the Electric Boat Division, builders of the Nautilus; and Navy Secretary Dan A. Kimball. *Courant file photo*

Left and below left: Presidential candidate John F. Kennedy speaks outside the Hartford Times Building in Hartford, on Nov. 7, 1960, one of his last campaign stops before Election Day.

Courant file photos

Above: Gov. Thomas J. Meskill presents his "State of the State" message to the state House and Senate on the General Assembly's opening day on Jan. 4, 1973. *Harry Batz / Hartford Courant*

Top left: Ella Grasso, elected the state's first female governor in 1974, delivers her budget address in 1979. *Mary Alice Dwyer / Hartford Courant*

Bottom left: Sen. Abraham A. Ribicoff, left, celebrates Rep. Christopher J. Dodd's Democratic nomination to the U.S. Senate in July 1980. Ribicoff, who was retiring after three terms in the U.S. Senate, nominated Dodd to succeed him. Dodd served five terms, the longest-serving U.S. senator in state history. *Judy Griesedieck / Hartford Courant*

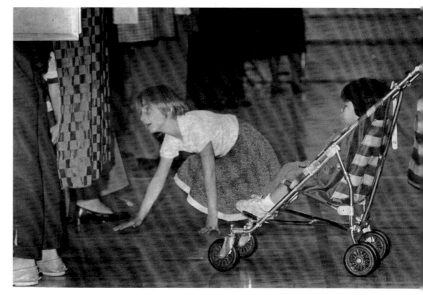

Above: First-time voter Charles Condon, left, is briefed on the use of the voting machine by Stella Niemis and Barbara Bigos in Harwinton on Election Day in 1980. *Jerry Williams / Hartford Courant*

Top right: A 1979-era voting machine in Torrington. *Courant file photo*

Bottom right: Donna Wasley peeks under the curtain of a voting booth at Robbins Junior High School in Farmington on Election Day in 1982. Robin Wasley looks on from the stroller.
Phil Farnsworth / Special to The Courant

Above: About 200 children, parents and youth service workers gather on the lawn of the state Capitol on April 4, 1980, to protest proposed cuts in the state Department of Youth Services' budget request. *Jerry Williams / Hartford Courant*

Above: Roman Catholic prelates join President Ronald Reagan on stage for his address to delegates to the Knights of Columbus convention at the Hartford Civic Center in August 1982. *Tony Bacewicz / Hartford Courant*

Above: Gov. Lowell P. Weicker Jr. gestures during a live television broadcast on Aug. 7, 1991. Weicker vetoed three budgets that did not include the income tax, and lawmakers held impassioned debates on what would become one of the most controversial political issues in state history. The political odyssey lasted much of the summer before dramatic votes in the state Senate and House of Representatives finally passed the income tax. The political wounds ran deep, and the issue was so draining that many lawmakers decided against seeking re-election in 1992. In January 1993, 67 of the 187 legislators were new arrivals — the highest number of freshmen legislators in the past 40 years. Weicker did not seek re-election and retired from politics. *Michael McAndrews / Hartford Courant*

Left: Thousands of protestors rally at the Capitol on Nov. 5, 1991, against the newly instituted state income tax. Police estimated a crowd of 40,000, but organizers said the number was closer to 70,000. *Michael McAndrews / Hartford Courant*

POLITICS AND PRISON

Left: Gov. John G. Rowland walks out of the side door of the Governor's Mansion in Hartford on June 21, 2004, to deliver his resignation address. Rowland, the state's 86th governor, was a shining prospect in national Republican politics who demonstrated a charismatic political mastery during a quarter-century political career until a corruption scandal led to a guilty plea that forced his resignation. He admitted taking more than $100,000 in bribes from businessmen looking for contracts or tax breaks. *Bob MacDonnell / Hartford Courant*

Below middle: Bridgeport Mayor Joseph P. Ganim leaves U.S. District Court in New Haven on March 19, 2003, moments after he was found guilty on 16 of 21 charges of public corruption. He served seven years in prison. *Patrick Raycraft / Hartford Courant*

Below right: T. Frank Hayes, the debonair former mayor of Waterbury who also had served part-time as state lieutenant governor, enters Wethersfield Prison in handcuffs in 1941. A year earlier, he and 22 others were convicted of conspiracy to defraud the city. *Hartford Courant archives*

Above: Under a blaze of television lights, the eight Connecticut members of the Electoral College gather around tables set up in the center of the Senate Chambers at the Capitol to cast their votes for president and vice president on Dec. 18, 1984. *Michael McAndrews / Hartford Courant*

Top left: Following a televised debate at The Bushnell in Hartford on Oct. 6, 1996, with Republican challenger Robert Dole and a post-debate rally at Hartford's Union Station, President Bill Clinton greets supporters. *Michael McAndrews / Hartford Courant*

Bottom left: Before making a rousing appeal at Central Connecticut State University for a higher minimum wage on March 5, 2014, President Barack Obama had lunch at the Cafe Beauregard in New Britain with, from left, Gov. Dannel Malloy, Massachusetts Gov. Deval Patrick and U.S. Labor Secretary Thomas Perez, as well as Vermont Gov. Peter Shumlin (not shown). *Richard Messina / Hartford Courant*

Below: President George W. Bush, the keynote speaker at the U.S. Coast Guard Academy's 126th commencement on May 23, 2007, waves to the family of graduate Michelle Robinett of Tolland. *Stephen Dunn / Hartford Courant*

COLORED SCHOOLS BROKEN UP, IN THE FREE STATES.

When schools have been established for colored scholars, the law-makers and the mob have combined to destroy them;—as at Canterbury, Ct., at Canaan, N. H., ... 10, 1835, at Zanesville and Brown Co., Ohio, in 1836.

BREAKING DOWN BARRIERS

The quest to topple the obstacles people have faced because of race, religion, ethnicity, gender or sexual identity has had a complex and often charged history in Connecticut.

It is a history that has forced the state to confront an ugly and long-suppressed fact: Connecticut was a slave state, much of its wealth tainted with the sweat and blood of slaves.

Thousands of slaves toiled in Connecticut in the 17th and 18th centuries. Connecticut's economy thrived thanks to the lucrative trade in meat, livestock, poultry, cheese, onions, corn, apples, candles, tobacco and whale oil — much of it shipped to slave plantations in the West Indies. Return shipments carried back sugar, molasses, rum, cotton — and slaves.

The Connecticut Courant routinely published notices about runaway slaves and slaves for sale.

And Connecticut's textile industry also prospered on the backs of thousands of slaves who picked cotton in the South.

Connecticut had been the second American colony, after Massachusetts, to pass a law recognizing slavery, in 1650, and it was the last state in New England to free its slaves.

Canterbury resident Prudence Crandall might now be acclaimed as the state heroine for opening New England's first school for black girls, but at the time in the early 1830s, her neighbors bullied and ostracized her, resorted to violence to try to destroy her school and went after her in the legislature and the courts.

Even so, Connecticut was a leading force in the abolition of slavery and sent thousands of young men to fight and die in the Civil War. Harriet Beecher Stowe's anti-slavery novel, "Uncle Tom's Cabin, or Life Among the Lowly," was a phenomenal best-seller that transformed how many Americans viewed slavery.

Connecticut was the first state to ratify the 14th Amendment to the U.S. Constitution, guaranteeing protection for people of all races and granting citizenship to "all persons born or naturalized" in the U.S., including former slaves.

The state also ratified the 15th Amendment in 1870, which granted citizens the right to vote, regardless of race, color or previous servitude. Women, however, were not included.

Then, after a half-century of protests and petitions, the 19th Amendment granted women the right to vote. Curiously, Connecticut was the 37th state to ratify the amendment — after ratification already was completed in 1920.

Connecticut's history of the struggle for equality also includes a chapter of virulent discrimination against the tens of thousands of Irish immigrants who fled the potato famine and arrived in Connecticut in the late 1840s and 1850s to work in factories, on railroads and in quarries here.

Connecticut grappled with race relations well into the 20th century, with riots in New Haven and Hartford.

And in the late 20th century and early 21st century, Connecticut took the lead in granting gay rights: In 1991, it was the fourth state to outlaw discrimination based on sexual identify; in 2005 it was the second state to legalize civil unions, and in 2008, following a state Supreme Court decision, the second to legalize same-sex marriage.

Opposite: The torching of Prudence Crandall's school, from The Anti-Slavery Almanac. *Prudence Crandall Museum*

BRAVING BIGOTRY, OPENING DOORS

Above: Prudence Crandall. *Prudence Crandall Museum*

Above right: Sarah Harris. *Prudence Crandall Museum*

The people of Canterbury didn't know what they were getting into in 1831 when they chose Prudence Crandall, an unmarried, 27-year-old teacher, to run the young ladies' academy in their town.

Crandall had hired a young African-American woman, Mariah Davis, as her "household assistant" and allowed her to sit in on classes. The father of Davis' fiance was the local agent for The Liberator, the abolitionist newspaper published by William Lloyd Garrison in Boston.

Davis loaned Crandall copies of the paper, in which, Crandall wrote, "the condition of the colored people both slaves and free was truthfully portrayed." She became even more committed to the movement to end slavery.

In 1832, when Sarah Harris, a 20-year-old woman who was soon-to-be Davis' sister-in-law, asked to study at the school, Crandall agreed.

Reaction was swift. The wife of an Episcopal minister told Crandall that if she continued to teach "that colored girl," the school could no longer be sustained by the community. "I replied to her," Crandall wrote, "that it might sink, then, for I should not turn her out!"

She wrote to Garrison, and proposed that if Canterbury would not support the school, she would advertise to "teach colored girls exclusively" and soon announced her planned school for "young Ladies and little Misses of color" in The Liberator. Some local businesses refused to trade with Crandall, the neighboring

doctor refused to treat her students' ills, and the town looked for legal ways to stop her. They also took their grievances to the legislature, getting a law passed — the "Black Law" — in May 1833 forbidding "any person" to "set up or establish in this state any school, academy or literary institution for the instruction of colored persons who are not inhabitants of this state."

A month later, Crandall was charged with violating the law. Three trials followed, with Crandall spending one night in jail. A lower-court conviction was overturned on a technicality in the Supreme Court of Errors, but this legal victory just turned the situation uglier. Horse manure was spread on the school's steps. Someone cut a cat's throat and hung the body on a gatepost. A rock was thrown through a window; Crandall calmly placed it on the mantel for all to see.

But the night of Sept. 9, 1834, ended Crandall's school. A mob armed with metal bars and clubs smashed windows and ransacked the ground floor. Crandall realized she was endangering her students' lives. She and her new husband announced plans to "abandon the school in that heathenish village," and let those involved in the attacks "have all the infamy and guilt which attach to the suppression of so praiseworthy an institution."

In 1886, the Prudence Crandall story had been revived and many hoped the Connecticut legislature would make restitution.

A Canterbury petition marking "the dark blot upon our fair fame and name" garnered 100 signatures. And the legislature awarded Crandall a $400-a-year restitution, for the remaining few years of her life. She died in 1890.

Crandall's legacy endured, and the arguments of her attorneys — that black Americans were citizens, that they could cross state borders to go to Crandall's school, if they wished — helped change the nation. Referring specifically to these arguments in the 1954 Brown v. Board of Education case helped NAACP lawyers win their own argument that African-Americans were entitled to go to the same schools as whites — not "separate but equal" schools.

An Escaped Slave In The Pulpit

James W.C. Pennington was 19 when he escaped slavery in Maryland and headed to Pennsylvania, where he learned to read. He was the first black student admitted to Yale University, though with the proviso that he sit in the back and not ask questions. Ordained as a Congregational minister, Pennington became pastor of Talcott Street Church in Hartford, now known as Faith Congregational Church, in 1840.

A contemporary of Harriet Beecher Stowe and Frederick Douglass, Pennington gained a reputation as a brilliant orator and zealous advocate for human rights, and often was invited to preach at other churches, including white churches. He represented Connecticut at an international convention on slavery held in London and earned an honorary doctorate from the University of Heidelberg in Germany.

After Congress passed the Fugitive Slave Act in 1850 and Pennington's former master took steps to recover his slave, John Hooker of Hartford, a direct descendant of Thomas Hooker and a brother-in-law of Harriet Beecher Stowe, purchased Pennington for $150. Hooker held the bill of sale for two days before turning it over to Pennington, saying he wanted to know what it felt like to own a doctor of divinity.

Left: James W.C. Pennington.

Hartford Courant archives

Right: John Brown.

Torrington Historical Society

John Brown On 'The Crime Of Crimes'

Though his attempt to incite a slave insurrection at Harpers Ferry, Va., failed, John Brown of Torrington succeeded in drawing national attention to the continuing plight of enslaved Americans.

When he was sentenced to death for treason on Nov. 2, 1859, he said: "I believe that to have interfered as I have done ... in behalf of His despised poor was not wrong, but right. Now, if it is deemed necessary that I should forfeit my life for the furtherance of the ends of justice, and mingle my blood with the blood of my children and with the blood of millions in this slave country whose rights are disregarded by wicked, cruel, and unjust enactments, I submit. So let it be done."

In his cell in late 1859, as he waited for his execution, Brown said he regarded slavery as "the crime of crimes," and the longer he lived, the more he hated it.

Top left: Minnie Hennessy of Hartford, a single, self-supporting businesswoman, was arrested for picketing with a suffrage banner at the gates of the White House on Oct. 6, 1917; her sentence was suspended. Arrested again two days later, she was sentenced to six months in prison at Occoquan Workhouse. *Harris & Ewing Photography / Library of Congress*

Top middle: Helena Hill Weed of Norwalk serves a three-day prison sentence in July 1917 for carrying a banner that read, "Governments derive their just powers from the consent of the governed." *Library of Congress*

Top right: Catherine Flanagan of Hartford, left, talks with national women's suffrage leader Alice Paul before presenting Connecticut's ratification of the 19th Amendment to the State Department in September 1920. *Library of Congress*

Right: Connecticut suffragists gathered in Hartford and Simsbury on July 13, 1918, to rally for women's voting rights and to ask President Woodrow Wilson to help get the 19th Amendment passed. *Hartford Courant archives*

Left: Women celebrate winning the right to vote as the 19th Amendment to the U.S. Constitution goes into effect on Aug. 26, 1920. *Hartford Courant archives*

Bottom left: A "Votes for Women" suffrage parade in Hartford, 1915. *Hartford Studies Project / The Connecticut Historical Society*

Bottom middle: Lillian Ascough of Hartford chaired the Connecticut branch of the Congressional Union for Woman Suffrage. *Library of Congress*

Bottom right: Catherine Flanagan of Hartford, at left, and Madeleine Watson of Chicago are arrested on Aug. 17, 1917, for picketing in front of the White House for women's right to vote with a banner that reads "How Long Must Women Wait For Liberty?" Both were sentenced to 30 days in the Occoquan Workhouse in Lorton, Va. Flanagan, then 28, was a state and national organizer for the National Woman's Party. When Connecticut ratified the 19th Amendment, she was asked to present the document to the U.S. secretary of state. *Harris & Ewing Photography / Library of Congress*

Opposite left: Demonstrators link arms and sing "We Shall Overcome" at a rally in July 1963.
Arthur J. Warmsley / Hartford Courant

Opposite top right: State members of the NAACP, college students and others parade in front of Grant's on State Street in Hartford in March 1960, to protest discrimination in the South by several chain stores that refused to serve blacks at lunch counters. *Harry Batz / Hartford Courant*

Opposite bottom right: Martin Luther King Jr. speaks on March 11, 1964, in Hartford to a closely packed crowd at ground-breaking ceremonies for Mount Olive Baptist Church's proposed housing project on Martin Street. King later invited the church's pastor, the Rev. Richard A. Battles Jr., who was the New England regional director of the Southern Christian Leadership Conference, to accompany him to Oslo, Norway, in December 1964 when he was awarded the Nobel Peace Prize. *Harry Batz / Hartford Courant*

Top left: Members of NECAP, the North End Community Action Project, stage a rally outside their headquarters at Clark and Nelson streets in Hartford in July 1963, calling on city officials to take action on problems in the city's North End.
Arman G. Hatsian / Hartford Courant

Top right: Thirman Milner of Hartford holds a sign during the historic March on Washington in August 1963. He later became the first black mayor of Hartford.
Harry Batz / Hartford Courant

Top left: The Windsor Market at Main and Pavilion streets is destroyed by fire and looted of groceries Aug. 5, 1968, during the second night of violence in Hartford after the assassination of Martin Luther King Jr. a day earlier. The market and the nearby Ben's Package Store were both white-owned businesses. *Maurice Murray / Hartford Courant*

Top middle: Hartford Public High School students attend an impromptu memorial service for King in Hartford on April 5, 1968. Students marched from Forest Street down Farmington Avenue to the Cathedral of St. Joseph for the brief memorial service. *Hartford Courant file photo*

Top right: Looters rush out of a drugstore at Albany Avenue and Garden Street in Hartford on April 5, 1968, a day after King's assassination. *Arman G. Hatsian / Hartford Courant*

Right: The Rev. Richard A. Battles Jr. of Mount Olive Baptist Church in Hartford addresses the congregation at an interfaith memorial service for the Rev. Martin Luther King Jr. on April 7, 1968, three days after King was assassinated. Battles was a close friend of the fallen civil rights leader. *Hartford Courant file photo*

Left: Protesters descended on the New Haven Green day after day in May 1970 and through much of the summer, questioning whether the "New Haven Nine" could get a fair trial. *Al Ferreira / Hartford Courant*

Bottom left: Fire at an old building on Church Street across from the New Haven Green draws crowds on May 3, 1970, and is a prelude to a confrontation between police and 200 demonstrators gathered for a rally for Black Panther Chairman Bobby Seale. *Al Ferreira / Hartford Courant*

Bottom middle: Black Panther Party Chairman Bobby Seale, one of nine Black Panthers charged in the slaying of Alex Rackley, is able to raise a clenched fist as he leaves the Montville Correctional Center in custody of a deputy sheriff for the first day of his trial in October 1970 in New Haven. The Black Panthers suspected that Rackley, a member of the Panthers, was an FBI informant. *UPI photo*

Bottom right: After an altercation between a Hartford policeman and four young men selling the Black Panther newspaper in front of a Main Street department store in August 1970, Hartford police lead some of the men they arrested into a van. *Harry Batz / Hartford Courant*

Above: Jacque Bennett of Portland rallies at the state Capitol against a measure under consideration in April 2005 to allow civil unions of same-sex couples.
Shana Sureck / Hartford Courant

Above: Victoria Lockyer, left, and DeeAnna Dederer leave Windsor Town Hall on Valentine's Day in 2012, after a civil ceremony declared them married. Connecticut legalized same-sex marriage in 2008. *Mark Mirko / Hartford Courant*

Opposite: Beth Kerrigan, left, recites her vows to partner Jody Mock during their wedding ceremony at their West Hartford home on Nov. 12, 2009, while their two boys, Carlos, left center, and Fernando look on. State Supreme Court Justice Richard Palmer, at right, presided over the ceremony. Kerrigan and Mock chose the one-year anniversary of the legalization of gay marriage in Connecticut, which was brought about by their landmark case, Kerrigan et. al. v. Commissioner of Public Health. Palmer, who wrote the majority opinion in the case, met Kerrigan for the first time only a month before the wedding when he was speaking about the case. Kerrigan, who was in the audience, was introduced to Palmer afterward and asked if he would preside at the wedding. *Cloe Poisson / Hartford Courant*

OUR STORMY HISTORY

When the first European settlers arrived in Connecticut in the 1600s, among the things they were unprepared for was the weather. Owing to its geographical location, their new home produced an array of meteorological varieties and extremes they could not have imagined. Sure, they had experienced cold and snow in Europe, but not this cold and snow.

The same could be said for thunderstorms, hurricanes, winds, unrelenting rains, summer hail, waves of scorching heat and tornadoes.

To make matters worse, the settlers arrived during the middle of what has been dubbed the Little Ice Age, a period marked by a temporary cooling of the Earth's temperatures that ran roughly from 1550 to 1750.

The Hurricane of 1635: The ocean surge from this Welcome-to-the-New-World storm in August caused the tide to rise to an unprecedented height in Boston and forced the Narragansett Indians to climb to the tops of trees to escape the water. The winds leveled forests and destroyed ships anchored along the Massachusetts coast, and there was a significant loss of life.

At the time there were still only a few settlers in Connecticut, which helped to limit the devastation from the storm, considered one of the five most devastating hurricanes ever to strike southern New England.

The Flood of 1692: Founded in 1634, Wethersfield slowly grew into an important shipping port owing to the fact that it was as far inland as large ships could navigate before the Connecticut River became too shallow. Business was so good that by 1692 six warehouses lined the banks of the river.

Then the river rose. Not only did the swift-moving water sweep away five of the six warehouses, it also opened up a deep-water shipping channel all the way into Hartford. The flood is most noted for creating what is now known as the Wethersfield Cove.

Winter 1717: The winter of "The Great Snow" had been so mild that in February people were planting beans and "comforting themselves with having gotten through the winter." Then, from Feb. 18 to 24, perhaps the greatest series of snowstorms in New England history struck, depositing 5 to 10 feet of snow across the region.

Left: Sharice Cannon makes her way home on unplowed North Street in Hamden on Feb. 12, 2013, after walking three blocks to a convenience store, two days after a blizzard dumped 40 inches of snow in her town. *Cloe Poisson / Hartford Courant*

Winter 1780: "The Hard Winter of 1780" began with snow on Nov. 2 and Nov. 17, followed by cold. Then, near the turn of the year, three massive nor'easters raged within a 10-day period, producing snow depths of 42 to 48 inches in the woods, while gale-force winds along the coast produced high tides and flooding. A period of extreme cold set in next with temperatures as cold as minus 20 degrees.

Sept. 22-23, 1815: The 1815 hurricane that punished New England, killing 38 and swallowing whole cities, began as a heavy rain, but eventually the wind blew so hard along the shore that buildings, fences, trees and boats were swept up. What the wind didn't take, the ocean did.

At Stonington a tide said to be 17 feet higher than normal washed across the town, taking everything on the wharves and the wharves themselves. A similar scenario took place in New London, where the surge flooded the city and then continued up the Thames River, not stopping until Norwich was under water as well.

Aug. 9, 1878: The Wallingford tornado of 1878 was remarkable for its severity. Nearly three dozen people were killed in a matter of minutes that hot summer August afternoon. Winds speeds were estimated at 207 to 260 mph.

March 11-14, 1888: The heavy snow, arctic temperatures, and winds of the Blizzard of 1888 caused an estimated 400 deaths. Connecticut was buried beneath several feet of snow. New Haven recorded 44.7 inches, Wallingford and Waterbury had 42 inches, Hartford 36 inches. Middletown took top honors, with 50 inches, a record that still stands. The strong, sustained winds caused massive snow drifts, so it was not uncommon for people to have to leave their homes through second-story windows. Cheshire recorded a 38-foot-tall drift, and in Bridgeport a 10-foot high drift extended for more than a mile.

The blizzard shut down every major city from Washington D.C. north through New England for up to a week. Still, most homes had heat (coal) and light (oil lamps).

Left: Outside the McDonough Hotel at Main and Court streets in Middletown after the Blizzard of 1888. *Middlesex County Historical Society*

Above middle: The train tracks in Forestville after the Blizzard of 1888. *The Connecticut Historical Society*

Above right: Wallingford residents in front of a badly damaged building following the deadly tornado that struck the town on Aug. 9, 1878. *Robert N. Dennis Collection, New York Public Library*

Left: The intersection of Main and Mulberry streets in Hartford.
William H. Lockwood / Connecticut State Library

Far left: Snow is piled high in front of a pharmacy on Main Street in Southington after the blizzard.
Southington Public Library

Below left: Horses cart snow to dump in the Park River after the Blizzard of 1888.
William H. Lockwood / Connecticut State Library

Below: Main Street in Hartford after the blizzard. *Hartford Courant file photo*

Above left: Flood waters submerge the Hotel Bond and other businesses on Asylum Street in Hartford, looking west, in March 1936. *F.F. Fisher / The Connecticut Historical Society*

Above right: An aerial view of Hartford in the 1936 flood. *National Archives*

Below: Front Street in Hartford sustained serious damage in the 1936 Flood. *The Connecticut Historical Society*

Summer 1911: As June 1911 melted into July, no one knew that an 11-day heat wave was on New England's doorstep. When it was done, it was responsible for more deaths than any other weather-related event. State reports show 71 deaths in Connecticut from the "effects of heat" in 1911; a 1997 analysis of the heat wave using a method called "total mortality" or "excess deaths," put the death toll in New England at 2,000.

The Flood of 1936: On March 9, a moisture-laden warm weather system moved up from the south and stalled. It rained for 13 days, and rivers and streams throughout Connecticut became raging torrents. Water and ice floes tore out bridges, highways, roads and railways. Worst off were Hartford and other towns along the Connecticut River as the river continued to rise to dangerous levels, especially past the month's midway point.

By March 19, the Connecticut reached the 30-foot mark. Bushnell Park was a lake. The Colt dike gave way and two people drowned. The next day, the river rose to 37.1 feet. As people forced to flee the floodwaters mobbed refugee centers, flood sightseers crowded the dry downtown area where vendors sold candy and peanuts.

By March 21, the Connecticut reached 37.56 feet, a record that remains. A fifth of Hartford was under water and some 10,000 people were displaced. Two more drownings were reported. Finally, late in the day the water began to recede. In the aftermath, leaders decided to build more dikes to contain the river. And they would build them, just not enough of them and just not quickly enough.

Left: An elderly woman is rescued in Hartford during the March 1936 flood. *Hartford Collection, Hartford Public Library / Hartford Studies Project*

Below left: A rowboat rescue on Temple Street in Hartford during the flood of 1936. *Jewish Historical Society / Hartford Studies Project*

Below right: A man walks on stilts in the Hartford flood waters in 1936. Photo is looking from the YMCA on Trumbull and Pearl streets. *Archives & Special Collections, University of Connecticut Libraries*

Top left: Katharine Hepburn sits amid the storm debris at her family's home in Fenwick. The cottage was washed away. *The Connecticut Historical Society*

Top right: Half-eaten by the sea, the remains of a house stand on White Sand Beach in Old Lyme. As the eye of the Hurricane of 1938 passed over Milford, land to the east was subjected to the storm's most powerful winds and waves. *Hartford Courant File Photo*

Right: Hurricane winds blew houses off their foundations, including this one in the Stony Creek section of Branford. *Willoughby Wallace Memorial Library*

Opposite top: Hurricane damage in Middletown. *Middlesex County Historical Society*

Opposite bottom: The flooded Park River passes under the brownstone bridge at Main Street in Hartford after the Hurricane of 1938. *The Connecticut Historical Society*

The Hurricane of 1938: The hurricane of Sept. 21, 1938, slammed into Long Island with such force that it registered on a seismograph in Alaska and washed windows in central Vermont with a salty spray.

The loss of life was estimated at 650 to 700 people, including 85 in Connecticut.

Damage from the storm included 19,500 structures damaged or destroyed; 26,000 vehicles dented or totaled; 5,600 boats wrecked, driven ashore or sunk; 20,000 miles of wires down; a half-million telephones out of service; 1,675 head of livestock and 750,000 chickens killed; half the tobacco crop rendered worthless; and enough trees toppled to build 200,000 five-room houses.

Monetary losses were put at $500 million in 1938 dollars, of which only 5 percent was covered by insurance.

Everyone who survived had a story, many of which have become part of Hurricane of '38 lore:

The man who left home for the post office to mail back a new barometer he thought was malfunctioning, only to find his house gone when he returned.

The sight of birds flying full force into the wind, and remaining in place.

Chestnuts being blown off a tree and peppering a nearby house like buckshot.

People standing on the beach looking at a strange fog bank rolling in only to realize as it gets closer that it is actually a wall of water traveling at highway speeds.

Hurricanes Connie and Diane: In August 1955, two hurricanes arrived within a week of each other. Together they drenched Connecticut with up to 20 inches of rain in some places.

The flood waters came on swiftly, and in the middle of the night. Most of those who died were taken by surprise. The highest concentrations of death and destruction were in Waterbury and the Unionville section of Farmington. Of the 29 people killed in Waterbury, 27 were from North Riverside Street, where 17 homes that had been next to the Naugatuck River vanished. River Glen, along the Farmington River in Unionville, had 38 homes scrubbed from the landscape; 12 of the town's 13 deaths occurred there.

It was the worst flooding in state history. The statewide death toll was 87, but some victims were never found. Curfews were imposed in many towns, and martial law declared. More than a dozen towns in the Naugatuck Valley, as well as Putnam in eastern Connecticut, were declared health hazards. All Waterbury residents were required to get a typhoid shot.

The total damage was estimated at $350 million to $400 million. Most homes were not covered by insurance.

Top: A truck charges through the flooded intersection of Main Street and Riverside Avenue in Bristol during the Flood of 1955. *SNET Collection, Archives & Special Collections at the Thomas J. Dodd Research Center, University of Connecticut Libraries*

Left: Viola Bechard is consoled by Ernest Kosswig of the East Farmington Volunteer Fire Department after learning that her 7-year-old daughter had been swept to her death in the River Glen section of Farmington in August 1955. *Robert B. Ficks / Hartford Courant*

Opposite: Main Street in Winsted after the 1955 flood. *National Archives*

Oct. 3, 1979: Although most tornadoes occur during June, July and August in Connecticut, the Windsor Locks tornado struck on Oct. 3, 1979. It set down at about 3 p.m., and quickly carved a corridor of death and destruction a quarter-mile wide and 4 miles long. Hardest hit was the Poquonock section near Bradley International Airport. Three people were killed and more than 300 injured.

July 10, 1989: The Hamden tornado of July 10, 1989, was the strongest of three tornadoes that formed in the northwest hills that day and went on a 60-minute, 70-mile tear before leaving the state. The strongest of the tornadoes swept through Hamden with wind speeds reaching 260 mph. About 400 structures were destroyed, 40 people were injured, and damage was put at $100 million.

Above left: Destroyed and severely damaged historic warplanes lie scattered at the Bradley Air Museum in Windsor Locks after the October 1979 tornado struck without warning. *John Long / Hartford Courant*

Above right: A member of the U.S. Weather Bureau staff launches a high-altitude weather balloon from the roof of the administration building at what was then know as Bradley Field in Windsor Locks in 1954. *Hartford Courant archives*

Opposite: Frank and Roberta Matthews survey the littered landscape around the foundation of their home on Oct. 6, 1979, two days after a tornado hit the Poquonock area of Windsor. *Stephen Dunn / Hartford Courant*

August 2011: By the time Hurricane Irene arrived on Connecticut's doorstep it had been downgraded to a tropical storm, a distinction lost on those along the coast being pounded by waves and wind. Although no shoreline community escaped unscathed, in the Cosey Beach area of East Haven 25 homes were destroyed, including four swept out to sea. Inland, there was widespread flooding.

Irene's toll in Connecticut included two dead, 132 homes destroyed, 35 communities declared disaster areas, and 830,130 without power.

October 2011: With leaves still on the trees as Halloween approached, the October snowstorm of 2011 sent limbs and branches across the state crashing into power lines and onto roads — plunging hundreds of thousands of people into darkness and making many roads impassable. The cleanup was slow and arduous as temperatures dropped and patience ran thin.

Eight people died in the aftermath of the freak storm, including four of the dozens of people who suffered carbon monoxide poisoning.

October 2012: Sandy was a Category 3 hurricane, then a post-tropical cyclone — the largest of its kind on record. With gale-force winds spanning 1,000 miles, Sandy reached as far west as Wisconsin and as far north as Canada.

In Connecticut, Sandy's storm surge was 9.83 feet above normal tide levels at Bridgeport, and 9.14 feet in New Haven. The National Hurricane Center attributed 72 deaths directly to Sandy, and another 87 tied indirectly to the storm. In Connecticut there were four deaths from the storm.

Feb. 9, 2013: The blizzard started slowly, with the first flakes falling in southeastern Connecticut about 8:30 a.m. on a Friday. Throughout the day, snow fell but the storm did not intensify until later, dropping 4 to 5 inches of snow an hour at its peak. Wind gusts topped 60 mph.

When residents awoke Saturday morning they were shocked to see as much as 3 feet of wind-driven, drifting snow surrounding their homes and cars. Hamden topped the snowfall totals, with 40 inches, and Milford was a close second at 38 inches. The storm was blamed for five deaths.

Above left: Huge waves slam into waterfront homes in Westbrook on Aug. 28, 2011. The wind intensity kept up long after the rain from Tropical Storm Irene disappeared. *Stephen Dunn / Hartford Courant*

Below left: Shayna Weinstein, left, gets a hug from her dad, Andy Weinstein, on Aug. 29, 2011, as they prepare to leave what's left of their summer cottage, at left, on Cosey Beach in East Haven after Tropical Storm Irene. *Cloe Poisson / Hartford Courant*

Above: The scene of damaged trees and downed power lines on Four-Mile Road in West Hartford is typical of the aftermath of the freak storm of heavy wet snow in October 2011.
Rick Hartford / Hartford Courant

Above: Houses on Cosey Beach in East Haven sustained serious damage from storm Sandy. *Michael McAndrews / Hartford Courant*

Above: Evonna Hellandbrand crosses the unplowed intersection of Lawrence and Grand Streets in Hartford after the February 2013 blizzard. *Brad Horrigan / Hartford Courant*

LAW AND DISORDER

T
ime has a way of dimming the true horror of some crimes.

So a woman like Amy Archer-Gilligan of Windsor — who blithely poisoned her husband and some of the elderly people in her care — later could become the subject of the comic play, "Arsenic and Old Lace."

And maybe we chuckle today that Joseph "Mad Dog" Taborsky, a wanton murderer who died in the electric chair in 1960, was nabbed in part by a footprint left by his size 12 shoe.

Their hideous actions have begun to fade into history.

Some people in trouble with the law actually win our admiration — the 18th-century counterfeiter Abel Buell of Killingworth, whose engraving skill helped him create the first map of the newly minted United States; the gutsy spinster sisters Abby and Julia Smith of Glastonbury, who refused to pay their taxes and became a rallying cry for women's suffrage; Yale University chaplain William Sloane Coffin, who stood with students opposed to the draft in 1968, refusing to desert them "in their hour of conscience."

But the shocking indifference and depraved brutality of many crimes never diminish, even when their victims and generations of their descendants are long gone.

And certain crimes sear themselves so deeply into the public's psyche that some images need almost no explanation:

The shattered glass of the entrance to Sandy Hook Elementary School.

A line of terrified children with their eyes closed, each one's hands on a classmate's shoulders, staggering away from their school.

A father looking heavenward, his eyes stretched open in grieving disbelief.

Left: Chris and Lynn McDonnell, whose daughter Grace was killed at Sandy Hook Elementary School on Dec. 14, 2012, are consoled outside the Sandy Hook fire station in Newtown. Gunman Adam Lanza killed his sleeping mother at home, then murdered 20 first-graders and six educators at the school before killing himself. It was one of the deadliest shootings in U.S. history. *Cloe Poisson / Hartford Courant*

ARTFUL COUNTERFEITERS

Though convicted of counterfeiting as a young man in 1764, Abel Buell of Killingworth went on to become an inventor and entrepreneur and, in 1784, to engrave the first U.S.-made map of the new United States.

Counterfeiting was a serious crime, in some cases punishable by death. The king's prosecutor, Matthew Griswold, who later became governor of Connecticut, must have taken a shine to the young engraver. Buell was sentenced to prison, cropping and branding, but he actually got off quite lightly. Only the smallest tip of Buell's ear was cropped, which he held on his tongue and managed to reattach. And the branding with a hot iron on his forehead was so high that he later could conceal the telltale mark with a lock of hair.

While in prison, Buell invented a stone-cutting machine, called a lapidary, and presented a gold ring with stones to Griswold. Shortly after receiving the gift, Griswold arranged for Buell's pardon.

Below left: Buell's map — decorated with illustrations of Minerva, the goddess of war, blowing a trumpet, and Liberty, holding a staff and a globe — was the first ever to display the Stars and Stripes. *Library of Congress*

Below right: Richard Brunton created an elaborate engraving of the infamous Old New-Gate Prison where he was sentenced to hard labor after his 1799 conviction for counterfeiting. *The Connecticut Historical Society*

Above: The lengthy trial of the Rev. Herbert Hayden, left, for the 1878 murder of Mary Stannard, a young North Madison woman who believed she was pregnant by him, ended in a hung jury. Hayden's wife, Rosa, right, attended the 17-week trial — then the longest in the state's history. Three decades later, the last surviving juror, Horace B. Perry of New Haven, told The Courant that the jury had not wanted to convict a man with such a beautiful wife. "The evidence, the eloquence of the array of legal talent and the cold charge of the judge counted little against the charm and magnetism of the wife of the minister accused of murder," Perry said. No one was ever convicted for killing Mary Stannard. *Courant file photos*

'LAST' HANGINGS

Above left: Hannah Occuish was just 12 years old when she was hanged in New London in 1786 for killing a 6-year-old who got her in trouble for taking some of her strawberries. Hannah was the last female criminal to be executed in Connecticut, and possibly the youngest person ever in the United States. *Hartford Courant archives*

Above right: Oliver Watkins, believed to have been driven to murder by a "temptress" named Waity Preston, was convicted of strangling his wife, Roxana, in 1829. Several thousand men, women and children turned out to watch Watkins hang in 1831. The raucous event in rural Brooklyn was the last public hanging in Connecticut. *Connecticuthistory.org*

Left: John Cronin, who killed his South Windsor employer at the breakfast table in 1893 because he was angry about a joke made at his expense, was the first man executed on the new automatic gallows at the new state prison in Wethersfield. *Courant archives*

Above: Abby and Julia Smith's refusal to pay when Glastonbury town fathers raised taxes for widows and unmarried women — but not for men — and the seizure of their cows by town officials thrust the two spinsters into the national limelight in the 1870s and made their case a rallying cry for the women's suffrage movement. *The Historical Society of Glastonbury*

'A MURDER FACTORY'

The Archer Home for Elderly and Indigent Persons in Windsor operated from the fall of 1907 until May 8, 1916, the day that state police arrived to question Amy Archer-Gilligan, search the home and ultimately arrest her for the murder of Franklin R. Andrews, a resident who had died two years earlier.

"Police Believe Archer Home For Aged A Murder Factory," read the lead headline in the next morning's Courant. Andrews' sister had become suspicious about her brother's death. She took her concerns about what was going on at the Archer home to the Hartford state's attorney and to Clifton L. Sherman, managing editor of The Courant.

Sherman, intrigued by what he was told and by other rumors he had heard about the Archer home, assigned Aubrey Maddock, the assistant city editor, to investigate what was happening in Windsor.

Using death certificates, Courant investigators determined that 60 people had died at the Archer Home since it opened. "Forty-eight of them, a number declared to be far in excess of the normal death rate at an institution of this kind, have been reported since January 1, 1911," The Courant reported.

The reporters also determined that Archer-Gilligan had purchased substantial quantities of arsenic at pharmacies in Windsor and Hartford, which she said was to deal with a rat problem.

Among the 60 people who had died at the Archer House was Archer-Gilligan's first husband, James Archer, and Michael Gilligan, who died less than three months after marrying Archer-Gilligan. The Courant presented its evidence to the governor, and state police began a quiet investigation. The remains of two of Archer-Gilligan's tenants were exhumed, including that of Andrews. Later, three more bodies were exhumed and revealed the presence of arsenic.

One of the people who followed Archer-Gilligan's trial in Hartford was playwright Joseph Kesselring, who was inspired to write his comic play "Arsenic and Old Lace."

The jury took only four hours to find Archer-Gilligan guilty, and she was sentenced to die by hanging on Nov. 6, 1917. Her lawyers appealed, and at her second trial, which began in Middletown on June 12, 1919, her lawyers mounted an insanity defense.

The trial came to an abrupt end on July 1, 1919, when Archer-Gilligan pleaded guilty to second-degree murder. She was sentenced to life in prison and began her sentence at the state prison in Wethersfield.

Five years later, Archer-Gilligan was declared insane. She spent the remaining 38 years of her life at Connecticut Valley Hospital in Middletown, where she died at age 94. The Courant reported: "Mostly she sat in a chair, dressed in a black dress trimmed with lace, a Bible on her lap, and prayed."

A DEBONAIR KILLER DIES CURSING

Left: Gerald Chapman in custody in 1925, after his capture for the killing of Officer James Skelly during a burglary in New Britain.

Boston Public Library / Leslie Jones Collection

On his third try, Gerald Chapman escaped from federal prison in Atlanta, where he was serving a 25-year sentence for a $2.4 million postal truck heist in New York — the largest armed robbery in the country at that time.

Chapman's audacious spirit and gentlemanly demeanor caught the public's fancy, and the press dubbed him "Public Enemy No. 1."

Then in October 1924, Chapman shot New Britain Police Officer James Skelly during a burglary of the Davidson and Levanthal department store. Skelly later died, but Chapman got away.

The eventual capture of Chapman in Muncie, Indiana, might not have happened without a clue turned up by then-Connecticut State Police Commissioner Edward J. Hickey.

While searching a Springfield office that housed Chapman's burglary tools, Hickey found an American Express Railway tag with a Muncie address written on it. The Courant called Hickey's clue "one of the most dramatic discoveries that has ever figured in the long and colorful annals of crime."

Hickey contacted authorities in Indiana, who apprehended Chapman and took him into custody after a brief shootout.

Connecticut wanted to try Chapman for killing Skelly, and federal authorities agreed to extradite him to Connecticut.

"Many in Connecticut and the rest of the country ... couldn't believe that Chapman, the class of the criminal world, could stoop to a petty burglary," The Courant wrote in a 1964 story about Connecticut's greatest trials.

Chapman was found guilty of murder — a crime punishable by death.

Letters poured in from around the country, urging that his life be spared. But shortly after midnight on April 6, 1926, Chapman entered the death chamber at Wethersfield State Prison.

As a guard put a black cap over his head, Chapman asked, "What are you putting that damn thing on me for?" The Courant reported.

Then while having his chin lifted, an angry Chapman said, "Take your damn hands off."

Chapman's cursing final words were not well-received.

"In this last act of his lurid life, those who knew him for what he was and had regarded him as but a nice little rat in a cage, concluded that he had acted true to form," The Courant wrote in a story that said Chapman "swore profusely as doom neared."

Despite the millions he had stolen, Chapman left behind no estate other than a pair of collar buttons and a book of synonyms.

SHIFTING VIEWS ON THE DEATH PENALTY

Joseph Taborsky — put to death on May 17, 1960, for terrorizing Connecticut during a three-month murderous robbery spree in the winter of 1956-57 — was the last man to die in Connecticut's electric chair.

Two years before Taborsky's crimes, Connecticut legislators debated a bill that sought to abolish capital punishment. The Courant backed the legislation after publishing a series of investigative stories that examined the death penalty, concluding, among other things, that there was no proof that execution was a deterrent to crime. Gov. Abraham Ribicoff also favored abolition at the time.

But then Taborsky and his accomplice, Arthur Culombe, struck.

The career criminals held up small businesses throughout the state in violent robberies that escalated into execution-style shootings of both owners and patrons.

Ribicoff changed his mind about wanting to end the death penalty. So did The Courant, writing in a Feb. 19, 1957, editorial just days before Taborsky and Culombe were arrested, that although the newspaper did not consider capital punishment a deterrent, executing "such cold killers is to remove a dangerous force from society, in the interest of protecting its members from further killings ... like putting out a fire, or killing a mad dog."

Right: Joseph "Mad Dog" Taborsky, right, shown after a 1957 court appearance, murdered six people, execution-style, in a string of robberies. *Courant file photo*

Right: Lorne Acquin leaves Waterbury Superior Court in July 1977, escorted by state police Trooper Marjorie J. Kolpa, after being arraigned on nine counts of murder. Until the 2012 Newtown shootings, Acquin's 1977 slaying of his foster brother's wife, their seven children and a young family friend in Prospect was the largest mass murder in Connecticut history. Acquin was sentenced to 105 years to life in prison, with the possibility of parole after 50 to 55 years. *Courant file photo*

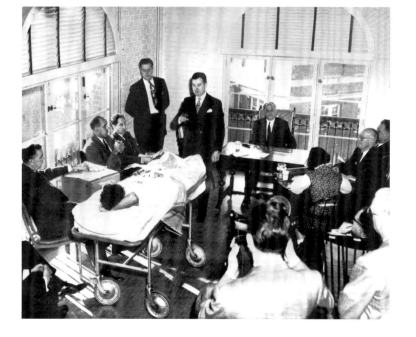

Left: A hospital room in New Britain becomes a courtroom on Dec. 27, 1951, when Frank Wojculewicz, on the stretcher, is arraigned on charges of killing a police officer and a bystander during a Nov. 5 holdup at a packing plant. Pointing a finger at Wojculewicz, who was paralyzed below the waist in the gun battle that followed, is Stanley Labieniec, foreman at the plant. Judge Harry Ginsburg sits at the desk in front of the window. Wojculewicz's attorney, Thomas F. McDonough, is seated at left. Wojculewicz was electrocuted in 1959 in a semi-prone position. *Courant file photo*

GRASSO'S REIGN OF TERROR

Above: Pallbearers carry the coffin of William Grasso from St. Michael's Church in New Haven after his funeral on June 21, 1989.
Joe Tabacca / Hartford Courant

Right: William Grasso lived in an unassuming ranch house and wore inexpensive clothes, but he dominated those around him and terrified his mob underlings. *Hartford Courant archives*

Not many people would consider a 10-year prison sentence a solid career move. But William P. Grasso wasn't like most people.

His cellmate was Raymond L.S. Patriarca, the snarling, Depression-era bootlegger who built his Patriarca crime family into the most powerful criminal organization in New England.

"Best thing that ever happened to me," Grasso later told an associate, "was when they sent me to Atlanta."

Grasso arrived in Atlanta as just another wiseguy from New England. He left as protégé and successor to one of the country's most powerful criminals. Unwittingly, the Department of

Justice made allies of two remarkably successful, reflexively brutal criminals, one at the top and one on the way up. For a time, the alliance would change the face of crime in Connecticut.

Grasso had always been a sputtering, spitting, seething cauldron of rage himself. His nickname was "The Wild Guy." Police records show his first arrest, in 1951, was for a petty assault. But it wasn't until his release from Atlanta in 1973 that he broke out of the limited role of rough New Haven thug. Terrifying long-established criminals, he seized big chunks of Connecticut and pushed into Western Massachusetts for the Patriarca family.

When Patriarca died of a heart attack in 1984, he was succeeded by his son, Raymond "Junior" Patriarca. Grasso, established as a criminal force of his own, became the family underboss, or second in command. But, FBI agents and mob associates regarded Grasso as the de facto boss, eclipsing the weak and retiring younger Patriarca.

Grasso operated in Boston and Providence through subordinates. But he was a hands-on boss on his own turf in Connecticut — until his own men, broken financially by his greed and terrified he would one day come gunning for them, turned on him.

His killers dumped his body in a patch of poison ivy by the side of the Connecticut River in Wethersfield.

But between his release from prison and his death in what became a civil war within the crime family, Grasso's elusiveness, his secrecy and his ability to shed surveillance made him an obsession of the FBI. The bureau never got him.

A WOOD CHIPPER AND DNA

Above: Richard B. Crafts is escorted by state police out of the Southbury Police station on Jan. 13, 1987, after his arrest at his home in Newtown. Based on evidence compiled by the state crime lab, Crafts was later convicted of murdering his wife, Helle Crafts, and disposing of her body with a wood chipper.

Joe Tabacca / Hartford Courant

Above: State police divers search the Housatonic River for remains of Helle Crafts.

Joe Tabacca / Hartford Courant

By the late 1980s, Dr. Henry Lee and his state crime lab were well-known, but a case that landed on his desk would make him an international sensation.

In late 1986, when some of Helle Crafts' friends reported she'd been missing for several weeks, her husband, Richard Crafts, initially told police he assumed his wife was visiting her family in Denmark. Police were suspicious of Crafts from the beginning, but without a body it seemed an impossible case to solve.

Then a highway worker who had noticed something strange while plowing the highway during a freak November snowstorm came forward. The plow driver told police he had seen someone with a wood chipper down on the banks of Lake Zoar early in the morning as he was plowing on I-84.

State police divers discovered a chain saw on the bottom of the lake. Lee analyzed it and determined there were blood specks in between the teeth. He also was able to recover the serial number from the chain saw, which had been damaged by being underwater. Investigators traced the chain saw to Richard Crafts.

Investigators scoured the shore of the lake and found less than 3 ounces of human remains, including a tooth with an unusual crown, a toenail covered in pink nail polish, bone chips and more than 2,600 bleached, blond human hairs.

Lee decided to try a new blood-typing technique called DNA testing to see whether he could determine if the remains were Helle Crafts'. The samples were too degraded to make a match, but the lab was able to ascertain that the blood was from a female with the same blood type as Helle Crafts.

The wood chipper case was likely the first criminal case in which DNA was used, but the case broke ground on a number of new techniques, including analysis of the striations on the wood chips, the rope fibers, bone analysis and fabric analysis.

The partial tooth with the dental crown intrigued Lee, who called in a dental expert to examine it. That turned out to be a key because it was determined the crown was likely installed by a dentist in Denmark, where Helle Crafts was from.

That was enough for the medical examiner's office to determine that Helle Crafts was dead, which paved the way for state police to arrest Richard Crafts on murder charges. It was the first time in the state's history a murder case would be tried without a body.

The first trial in New London ended in a mistrial when one juror refused to deliberate anymore and walked out of the courthouse. Crafts was convicted at a second trial and is still serving a 50-year prison sentence.

The salacious details of the wood chipper murder garnered international media attention, and Connecticut's forensic science guru became a highly sought-out expert.

Above: Dr. Henry Lee, shown discussing the JonBenet Ramsey case in 1999, opened his first crime lab in a converted bathroom at the state police barracks in Bethany in 1979. In 1990, Lee opened the high-tech, 74,000-square-foot state police lab in Meriden, which since has developed into 240,000 square feet of forensic laboratory space.

Joanne HoYoung Lee / Hartford Courant

Left: George Reardon, an endocrinologist from West Hartford, used a so-called growth study he ran at St. Francis Hospital and Medical Center from the 1960s to 1990s as a pretext to sexually abuse and take obscene photographs of hundreds of children. The explicit photographs — discovered behind a false wall at his former house after his death in 1998 — led to hundreds of lawsuits against the hospital, though he was never charged. *Michael McAndrews / Hartford Courant*

Right: Arne Johnson, who was convicted of the 1981 stabbing death of Alan Bono, claimed he was possessed by the devil at the time of the killing. It was the first time in the United States that someone tried to use demonic possession as a defense. *Anacleto Rapping / Hartford Courant*

Below: Young Puerto Rican militants called Los Macheteros stole $7 million from a Wells Fargo depot in West Hartford in 1983, declaring they would use it in their war for independence. It was, at the time, the largest cash robbery in U.S. history. The money and Victor Gerena, the Wells Fargo inside man from Hartford who took it, have never been found. *Hartford Courant archives*

FBI TEN MOST WANTED FUGITIVE

BANK ROBBERY; UNLAWFUL FLIGHT TO AVOID PROSECUTION – ARMED ROBBERY; THEFT FROM INTERSTATE SHIPMENT

VICTOR MANUEL GERENA

Photograph taken in 1983   Photograph retouched   Computer Age Enhanced Photograph

Aliases: Victor Ortiz, Victor M. Gerena Ortiz

The Hartford Courant.

A Deadly Grievance

Worker Kills 4 Bosses, Self At Lottery Site

The Scene: Panic And Death

The Gunman: An Angry Friend, A Withdrawn Colleague

Right: Alex Kelly is escorted out of Stamford Superior Court in July 1997 after being sentenced to 16 years in prison for the 1986 rape of Adrienne Bak. Kelly of Darien was 18 when he forced himself on Bak, then 16. He fled the country before his trial and was a fugitive for eight years, on an international run that police say his parents helped finance. After he was convicted, Bak went public with her story, in hopes that it would help other women who have been raped counter their feelings of shame and regard themselves as survivors.

Cloe Poisson / Hartford Courant

Left: Following the death of 94-year-old Ottilie Lundgren from anthrax poisoning in November 2001, state and federal investigators process evidence outside her Oxford home. A phone bill removed from her house is in the zipped plastic bag. Bruce E. Ivins, an anthrax expert at the U.S. Army Medical Research Institute of Infectious Diseases, killed himself in 2008 as authorities were getting ready to indict him for the anthrax attacks, which claimed the lives of five people and changed the way mail is handled. The FBI's investigation of the attacks remains under investigation.

Stephen Dunn / Hartford Courant

Above: Angry about an unresolved grievance over his job duties and pay, Matthew Beck methodically executed four people at state lottery headquarters in 1998 before killing himself. At the time it was the deadliest workplace slaughter in the state's history. The Courant won a Pulitzer Prize for its breaking news coverage of the rampage.

Above: Serial killer Michael Ross appears in a Dec. 15, 2004, video of a court-ordered psychiatric examination conducted at the Osborn Correctional Institution in Somers after he waived his right to continue to appeal his death sentence. Ross, who was convicted of kidnapping and strangling four young women and admitted killing four others, was put to death by lethal injection at Osborn on May 13, 2005, the first person to be executed in New England in 45 years.
Hartford Courant archives

Above right: Edwin Shelley gets a hug from his wife, Lera, shortly after 3 a.m. on May 13, 2005, after speaking with the press about witnessing the execution of Michael Ross, who murdered their 14-year-old daughter Leslie on Easter Sunday in 1984. At right is state Attorney General Richard Blumenthal.
Stephen Dunn / Hartford Courant

Left: Steve Riege of Hartford and Rachel Lawler of Cheshire protest against the death penalty in the "Gallows to Gurney" walk on May 12, 2005. Numerous demonstrators both for and against the death penalty turned out as Michael Ross' execution neared. *Patrick Raycraft / Hartford Courant*

Above: Dr. William J. Petit Jr. talks with the media in October 2011, after jurors found Joshua Komisarjevsky guilty of all 17 charges in the deaths of Petit's wife, Jennifer Hawke-Petit, and their daughters, Hayley and Michaela, during the July 23, 2007, Cheshire home invasion. Petit is flanked by his late wife's parents, MaryBelle Hawke and the Rev. Richard Hawke, at left, and by his sister, Johanna Petit Chapman, right. Career criminals Komisarjevsky and Steven Hayes both remain on death row for the home invasion crimes. State lawmakers repealed the death penalty in 2012 but insisted that inmates already on death row remain eligible for execution. *Mark Mirko / Hartford Courant*

The newspaper front page:

AMERICA'S OLDEST CONTINUOUSLY PUBLISHED NEWSPAPER

Hartford Courant

VOLUME CLXXVI NUMBER 352   COURANT.COM • MOBILE.COURANT.COM   MONDAY, DECEMBER 17, 2012

He spoke for a nation in sorrow, but the slaughter of all those little boys and girls turned the commander in chief into another parent in grief, searching for answers.

'THEY ARE ALL OUR CHILDREN'

Police Presence At Schools In State Will Be Increased

By ALAINE GRIFFIN and AMANDA FALCONE
agriffin@courant.com

Children returning to classes across Connecticut Monday will see uniformed police officers in and around their schools as officials grapple with how to handle concerned parents and anxious students following the massacre Friday at Sandy Hook Elementary School in Newtown.

School administrators over the weekend posted on school district websites instructional videos and psychologists' tips on how to talk to their children about violence in anticipation of what's expected to be a tough day for many schools and their students.

Officials said they hope the increased police patrols and heightened safety awareness will not raise the anxiety of children already struggling with details they may know about the killings.

"I know Friday was one of the toughest for school superintendents, the worst nightmare any of us could fathom," Cheshire Schools Superintendent Greg J. Florio said Sunday. He said he expects Monday to be just as rough, similar to the day children first returned to school after the Sept. 11 terrorist attacks.

"It's kind of a fine balance we have to keep," Florio said. "You know that people are aware of the situation but you want to have as much of a sense of normalcy as you can."

By the time the school bell rings Monday morning, some school staff members will already have met to discuss security and other issues related to Friday's shooting. Other meetings took place over the weekend and included input from parents and residents without students.

Students at several schools will see

POLICE, A12

Sending Them Out The Door Will Never Feel The Same

Monday morning, parents must do what for many will still feel excruciating.

Send their children to school. And try not to worry.

What a regrettable milestone. The safest place isn't that safe at all.

Locked doors, intercom buzzer systems, a cop in every high school and millions of dollars in security improvements cannot stop the terrorists who live among us.

I watched Sunday as the ubiquitous Lt. J. Paul Vance promised us schools will be safe. I listened as a leading educator said we are all at risk. A school security expert told me it's the world we live in now.

One administrator who remembers the feeling after Columbine told me he, too, is anxious about Monday morning, the first school day after things changed.

This Monday morning, police officers will be among the first to welcome children back at schools throughout Connecticut. It is the horrible new normal.

"Our hearts are broken, but our hands are extended," state Education Commissioner Stefan Pryor said.

He spent Sunday meeting with educators from Sandy Hook Elementary, the first time teachers had come together since Friday's tragedy.

Pryor said the state has brought in a special consultant, David Schonfeld, director of the National Center for School

RICK GREEN
COLUMNIST

GREEN, A11

Charlotte Bacon • Daniel Barden • Rachel Davino • Olivia Engel • Josephine Gay • Ana Marquez-Greene • Dylan Hockley • Dawn Hochsprung • Catherine Hubbard • Chase Kowalski • Nancy Lanza • Jesse Lewis • James Mattioli • Grace McDonnell • Anne Marie Murphy • Emilie Parker • Jack Pinto • Noah Pozner • Caroline Previdi • Jessica Rekos • Avielle Richman • Lauren Rousseau • Mary Sherlach • Victoria Soto

'This Little Girl Could Light Up The Room'

Family, friends and co-workers remember the 20 children and seven adults killed in Newtown. Photos of Madeleine Hsu, Benjamin Wheeler and Allison Wyatt were not available.

Story, Pages A6, A7 and A8

Obama Offers Comfort, Vows To Address Gun Violence

By DANIELA ALTIMARI
daltimari@courant.com

NEWTOWN — A somber President Obama told a shattered community that the nation has let its children down.

"We're not doing enough," Obama said during an interfaith service at Newtown High School on Sunday night. "And we will have to change. Since I've been president, this is the fourth time we have come together to comfort a grieving community torn apart by mass shootings, [the] fourth time we've hugged survivors, the fourth time we've consoled the families of victims."

The president's 18-minute speech was more about providing comfort to the emotionally fragile citizens of Newtown than about laying out his legislative agenda on gun control. However, he made clear his intentions to seek a new path to end gun violence.

Obama pledged to "use whatever power this office holds" to engage law enforcement, mental health professionals, parents and teachers in an effort to reduce gun violence.

"We can't accept events like this as routine," Obama said. "Are we really prepared to say that we're powerless in the face of such carnage, that the politics are too hard? Are we prepared to say that such violence visited on our children year after year after year is somehow the price of our freedom?"

Obama spoke to about 800 people in an auditorium located less than a half-mile from Sandy Hook Elementary School, where six adults and 20 children were killed in one of the worst mass shootings in the nation's history. Another 1,200 or so gathered in the high school gymnasium to watch a video feed of the service.

A wave of heavy sobs could be heard throughout the auditorium when Obama listed the names of the slain teachers, school psychologist and school principal. Those sobs were audible when he concluded his comments by saying the first names of the 20 slain children.

OBAMA, A4

A SUNDAY OF SORROW

GUN CONTROL: Some of the state's congressional representatives called for a national discussion on gun control. Page A4

SAFETY SHATTERED: A Sandy Hook resident wonders what it will take to restore the town's sense of community. Page A13

REMEMBERING: Thousands of grief-stricken mourners gathered in churches across Connecticut to remember the children and adults killed in Newtown. Page A10

NANCY LANZA: Friends said Nancy Lanza spoke proudly of her sons, but her home life was off limits. Page A11

FUNERALS: Funeral services have been scheduled for many of the victims. Page B3

HUSKIES PAUSE: The UConn men will observe a moment of silence before their game Monday night. Page C1

ONLINE: Visit courant.com/newtownshooting for more on the story, including video and photos.

$1.00 Copyright 2012 The Hartford Courant Co.

CLASSIFIED C5, C6 • MOVIES D3 • COMICS D4, D5 • PUZZLES D5 • LOTTERY A2 • SPORTS C1

Above: Ginna Ortiz of New Canaan cries as Veronique Pozner, mother of Sandy Hook victim Noah Pozner, speaks at a rally against gun violence at the state Capitol in February 2013. *Mark Mirko / Hartford Courant*

TRAGEDY AND RECOVERY

One of the first big breaking news stories The Courant published was about a tragic fire that left six people dead and 20 injured.

The General Assembly had proclaimed May 23, 1766, "as a day of general rejoicing" after the British Parliament repealed the Stamp Act of 1765, which had required, among other things, that Colonial newspapers use stamped paper from England at a hefty tax. A fireworks extravaganza was planned as part of the Colonial celebration.

"Sudden was the transition from the height of joy to extreme sorrow," Courant publisher Thomas Green wrote in his account that ran on Monday, May 26. When the canisters of fireworks were delivered, bits of gunpowder spilled along a trail leading to the brick schoolhouse where the fireworks were being prepared. Several neighborhood boys "undesignedly and unnoticed set fire to the scattered powder, which soon communicated to that within doors and in an instant reduced the building to a heap of ashes."

In a testament to his journalistic skills, Green was able to list everyone killed and wounded in the inferno, including each one's occupation, family ties and extent of injuries — and then set the type by hand in time for Monday's paper.

Tragedies of every imaginable variety have tested Connecticut in the two and half centuries since — collapsing infrastructure, train wrecks, crashes, explosions, fires, natural disasters, epidemics, deadly weather, terrorist attacks, hideous crimes and terrible personal losses that have gripped the public.

Through anguish, heartbreak and sometimes unspeakable pain, the people of Connecticut have coped and comforted one another, planting gardens, building hospitals and playgrounds, starting foundations, advocating for political change, joining in runs and rides, lighting candles and embracing one another in an effort to heal great hurt. The hum of loss never goes away, but they have honored lost loved ones, they have forgiven, they have found the strength to carry on.

Left: Naval corpsman Milton Villa, right, plays taps after the names of each of the Connecticut residents who died in the attacks on Sept. 11, 2001, are read at the annual memorial service at Sherwood Island State Park in Westport on Sept. 10, 2014. The Marine color guard includes, from left, Sgt. Joshua Rivera, Sgt. Andres Santos, Sgt. Jordan Harrison, Gunnery Sgt. William Pieczarka and Villa.
Patrick Raycraft / Hartford Courant

AWAKENING TO INDUSTRIAL INJURIES

An explosion at the Fales & Gray Car Works on Potter Street near Hartford's riverfront on the afternoon of March 2, 1854, wasn't caused by a leaky old boiler but a new one that had been in operation for only about a month. Nine people died instantly, 10 or 12 more died later, and as many as 50 people were injured.

At the time, the city had few resources for dealing with such a large number of casualties. Two weeks later, The Courant called for the city to build a hospital.

"The late unfortunate calamity demonstrates clearly the necessity of the establishment of a regular and efficient Hospital in our City. ... Accidents are constantly occurring in the breaking of limbs and in other similar calamities where a place is needed for the proper atten-

tion and care of those suffering thereby. ... The utility of such an institution is evident. The necessity of it so great as to call for immediate action. Who will move in it?"

On May 2, 1854, just two months after the explosion, a grass-roots group formed a committee to found a hospital in Hartford. The state legislature passed a resolution later that year incorporating Hartford Hospital.

Above: The Fales & Gray Car Works in Hartford, which employed about 300 people, was nearly completely destroyed by an exploding steamboiler. *Hartford Courant archives*

Left: The Colt Armory's East Armory in Hartford, which was manufacturing pistols and revolving rifles during the Civil War, burned to the ground on Feb. 4, 1864. One man died and 900 people were left out of work. Confederate sympathizers were rumored to have started the fire, but no cause was ever determined. *Tomas J. Nenortas Collection*

'THE DAY THE CLOWNS CRIED'

It was an ordinary day that turned into a horrific tragedy in a matter of minutes. In the midst of World War II, on July 6, 1944, the Ringling Bros. and Barnum & Bailey Circus provided a welcome diversion in Hartford.

Less than half an hour into the show, the big top suddenly caught fire, an inferno that destroyed the tent in just 10 minutes.

The mammoth tent had been waterproofed with a mixture of 6,000 gallons of gasoline and 1,600 pounds of paraffin — a flammable formula that had been used for decades.

Some in the audience were so intent on watching the Flying Wallendas perform on the high wire above the center ring that the shouts of "Fire!" didn't register at first. Others sat mesmerized by the sight of thundering flames and smoke.

Panicked crowds mobbed the exits, knocking over chairs that blocked the way out for many others before the tent collapsed.

But others were courageous and heroic. One boy who cut his way out of the tent with a fishing knife then cut his way back into the tent to rescue an older man he had seen and also saved a 4-year-old girl who had been trampled.

The fire killed 168 people, many of them children, and injured nearly 700 among the 6,000 spectators. It also left haunting, terrifying memories for many of the survivors.

Above: Famed circus clown Emmett Kelly carries a bucket of water during the Hartford circus fire. *The Connecticut Historical Society*

Far left: Smoke billows from the big top on July 6, 1944. *Courant file photo*

Left: Many of the spectators at the circus were mothers and children. Some of those killed have never been identified. *Courant file photo*

Right: A fire that started inside the walls destroyed the Cathedral of St. Joseph in Hartford on Dec. 31, 1956, leaving it an unsalvageable ruin. Flames were discovered behind the main altar just after the 7 a.m. Mass. It took 300 firefighters eight hours to subdue the fire. A day earlier a fire destroyed St. Patrick's Church on Church Street, prompting suspicions of arson. *Hartford Courant archives*

Below: Two firemen at a side entrance look on as hose lines continue to pour water into the smoldering cathedral on Jan. 2, 1957. A new cathedral was dedicated at the site of the fire on May 15, 1962. *Hartford Courant archives*

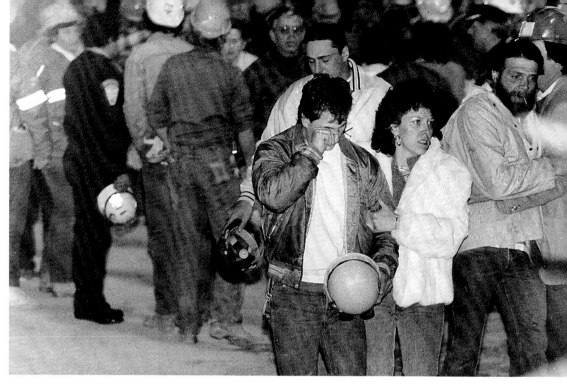

Above: A construction worker wipes his tears as he leaves the L'Ambiance Plaza site after a memorial service on May 2, 1987, for workers killed there. *Michael Lennahan / Hartford Courant*

Below right: In 1989, Christina Paternostro weeps at the memorial to the victims of the L'Ambiance Plaza disaster two years earlier, including her husband, Guiseppe Paternostro. *Albert Dickson / Hartford Courant*

Above: L'Ambiance Plaza, a residential apartment building under construction on Washington Avenue that many hoped would spur further development in Bridgeport, suddenly collapsed the afternoon of April 23, 1987, killing 28 construction workers. The next day, a crane lowers rescue workers into the rubble of the collapsed building site. *Cloe Poisson / The Hartford Courant*

Right: Family members of L'Ambiance Plaza victim Vincent Figliomeni and others mourners walk to a service at the site of the collapse. *John Long / Hartford Courant*

Above: Garner Lester of Redding comforts Vera Knapp of the Congregational Church of Easton at a memorial service on Sept. 11, 2001, for Peter and Sue Kim Hanson and their daughter Christine, who were passengers on United Airlines Flight 175 that crashed into the World Trade Center. Peter Hanson grew up in Easton.

Patrick Raycraft / Hartford Courant

Above: Brez Ebner, 6, of Wethersfield holds his candle aloft on the Broad Street Green in Wethersfield on Sept. 8, 2002, during a candlelight ceremony remembering 9/11.

Rick Hartford / Hartford Courant

Above left: At a memorial service at Sherwood Island State Park in September 2011 to commemorate the 10th anniversary of 9/11, Carolyne Hynes and her daughter Olivia, 9, of Weston, place flowers on the marker of her husband and Olivia's father, Thomas Hynes, who was killed in the attacks. Hundreds of victims' family members and friends and state officials attended the ceremony and visited the memorial, where the names of Connecticut's 153 victims are engraved. *Stephen Dunn / Hartford Courant*

Above right: At the 10th anniversary remembrance, Mary Henwood touches the name of her son, John Christopher Henwood, who was killed on 9/11. The wall sculpture is designed with a canopy of flowers made from aluminum salvaged from the World Trade Center towers. *Stephen Dunn / Hartford Courant*

Left: On the fifth anniversary of the attacks of Sept. 11, 2001, University of Connecticut sophomores Erin Considine, left, and Allison Demanosow keep their candles lit during a vigil. *Tia Ann Chapman / Hartford Courant*

Right: Thousands of law enforcement officers from around New England and New York stand outside the Holy Spirit Church in Newington on Jan. 4, 2005, during the funeral of Newington Police Officer Peter Lavery, who was shot to death in the line of duty responding to a domestic disturbance.

Stephen Dunn / Hartford Courant

Below: In July 2005, a dump truck that went out of control when its brakes failed collided head-on with a bus and 18 other vehicles at the bottom of Avon Mountain. The crash killed four, including the truck driver, and injured 20.

Shana Sureck / Hartford Courant

Left: After living with intense anger, the Rev. Walter Everett came to forgive the man who killed his son in 1987, and the two men now make appearances together to speak about forgiveness and justice. *Mark Mirko / Hartford Courant*

Opposite: Luminaria are set out around the First Congregational Church in the center of Cheshire in November 2010 during the annual Lights of Hope in honor of the slain members of the Petit family.

David Butler II / Special to The Courant

Above: Nelba Marquez-Greene, who lost her daughter Ana-Grace in the 2012 Newtown massacre, listens to recommendations from members of the Sandy Hook Advisory Committee in November 2014. *Michael McAndrews / Hartford Courant*

Above left: A woman and a little girl leave a bouquet of flowers at a makeshift memorial near Sandy Hook Elementary School on Dec. 15, 2012, one day after Adam Lanza stormed the school and killed 26 people, including 20 children. *Cloe Poisson / Hartford Courant*

Left: From left, Molly Holmstead, Will Checketts and Gabe Checketts, all from Darien, fit their hands into handprints made by family members of Emilie Parker in a cement marker at Emilie's Shady Spot playground at Riverside Park in New London during the dedication ceremony in November 2013. The playground is one of several built in memory of children who died at Sandy Hook Elementary School. *Cloe Poisson / Hartford Courant*

Opposite: Lee Paulsen listens during a healing service held at St. John's Episcopal Church in the Sandy Hook section of Newtown on Dec. 14, 2012. *Cloe Poisson / Hartford Courant*

OUR STARRING ROLES

The arts in Connecticut got off to a rather inauspicious start, in remarkable contrast to today's flourishing and vibrant diversity. During the Colonial and Revolutionary days, Connecticut's people did most of their singing in church, debating for decades the proper way to intone the hymns to most effectively praise the Almighty.

As for musical instruments, they were forbidden in church, and a few early Connecticut lawmakers sought to ban instrumental music altogether.

Until late in the 18th century, there also was little public entertainment.

Anyone who dared to put on a professional show, which was rare, was careful to stress its wholesomeness. A theater ad in The Courant in 1795 pointed out the producers' intention to uplift: "They beg leave to offer their assurances that everything in their power will be studied that they may tend to render the entertainments a source of moral instruction as well as amusement."

During a four-year period in the 1790s, 200 shows were presented at the New Theatre on Temple Street. But the curtain came down in 1800 when the legislature banned "theatrical shows and entertainments" and "painted vanities," imposing a $50 fine on anyone who exhibited or aided in exhibiting "any tragedies, comedies, farces or other dramatic pieces or compositions." The theater in Hartford was turned into a Sunday school.

Things changed a half-century later when the legislature allowed each town to "regulate its own amusements," and by 1855, "Uncle Tom's Cabin," based on the wildly popular 1852 novel about slavery by Hartford's Harriet Beecher Stowe, was performed in the city.

The austerity toward music soon gave way as well, and performance of music in the state rapidly flowered through the 19th century. Even the smallest towns formed bands for parades and holiday celebrations, and singing societies sprang up.

Musical instruction became a badge of cultivation, especially for young women. And churches relaxed their early prohibitions and became important centers of musical performance. Hartford's First Church of Christ, known today as Center Church, established a formal concert series as early as 1822, which survives to this day, nearly 200 years later.

There wasn't a theater in New Haven until the 1870s; the first was the Music Hall that later became the Grand Opera. For decades, until the Shubert Theater opened in 1914, music was the prime focus, not drama. While the Elm City was slower to embrace stage shows, the state's first all-professional orchestra — only the fourth in the country — made its debut in New Haven in 1894.

In the 20th century, Connecticut's musical life took on a more cosmopolitan tone. One development in particular suddenly, and almost single-handedly, lifted Connecticut out of its somewhat provincial status — the opening of the grand, 2,800-seat Bushnell Memorial Hall in 1930. It hosted virtually every important classical musician, singer, ensemble and conductor in the world, as well as touring theatrical shows that could attract thousands.

Left: A formally dressed audience awaits a performance at Bushnell Memorial Hall in Hartford in 1931, a year after the Art Deco-style auditorium opened. *Hartford Courant archives*

Right: Hartford native Katharine Hepburn, right, with Milton Stiefel, producer at the Ivoryton Playhouse, where Hepburn performed a series of plays in the early 1930s. Hepburn started her career on stage and caught people's attention with her elegant, brainy demeanor, but she often was overwhelmed by nerves. By 1932 she began her film career, and in the movies her nerves and mistakes were less of a problem, and filmmakers could capture her unconventional beauty up close. *Hartford Courant archives*

Below: The U.S. Postal Service unveils the Katharine Hepburn postage stamp as part of the Legends of Hollywood series on May 12, 2010, which would have been her 103rd birthday, at a ceremony at the Katharine Hepburn Cultural Arts Center in Old Saybrook with, from left, filmmaker Anthony Harvey, U.S. Postmaster General John Potter, actor Sam Waterston and Chuck Still, executive director of the center. *Richard Messina / Hartford Courant*

Above: In the late 19th and early 20th centuries, there wasn't a bigger star on stage than William Gillette. The Hartford native, pictured in 1929, was best known for his portrayal of Sherlock Holmes; he performed the role more than 1,300 times. When he played Holmes in 1900, The Courant wrote, "Many proclaim him the most finished and polished actor of the day, the acme of realism." The Courant also reported that author Booth Tarkington wrote to Gillette of his performance, "I would rather see you play Sherlock Holmes than be a child again on Christmas morning." *Hartford Courant archives*

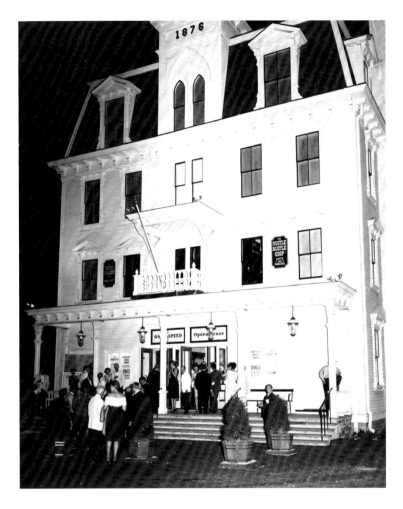

Left: Actress Rosalind Russell, who grew up in Waterbury, performs in "Auntie Mame." *Corbis Images*

Below: "Boomerang!" a 1947 film noir directed by Elia Kazan, told the true story of the 1924 slaying of a priest in Bridgeport. A suspect was arrested, but state's attorney Homer Cummings believed he had been railroaded, so he demolished his own case and set the suspect free, shocking the state. The movie, starring Dana Andrews as Henry Harvey, a fictionalized version of Cummings, was shot in Stamford. Officials in Bridgeport, still embarrassed about the case, refused Kazan permission to shoot there. *Hartford Courant archives*

Above: William Goodspeed opened the Goodspeed Opera House on the Connecticut River in East Haddam in 1877, bringing shows to Connecticut on his steamboat line. The eclectic building combined commerce — including a general store, post office and dentist's office — with the arts. But the performances declined after his death, and in 1902 the venue stopped presenting shows. Six decades later, after a three-year restoration, the Goodspeed reopened for performances in 1963 and has been presenting musicals ever since. Here, patrons gather for an opening night in 1963. *Goodspeed Musicals*

Right: Actor Paul Newman listens to a question after announcing plans to create a summer camp for children with life-threatening illnesses at a press conference at Yale-New Haven Hospital on Sept. 17, 1986. The Hole In The Wall Gang Camp opened in Ashford in 1988. *Michael Lennahan / Hartford Courant*

Below: Actors and longtime Westport residents Joanne Woodward and Paul Newman answer questions at the Westport Country Playhouse in May 2002, after an announcement that Paul Newman would star in the upcoming production of "Our Town." Woodward, who saved the playhouse after it fell into serious disrepair, served as the theater's artistic director from 2000 to 2005. *Richard Messina / Hartford Courant*

Above: "The Frogs," a 1974 Yale Repertory Theatre production, adapted from the ancient comedy by Aristophanes, was performed in the swimming pool of Yale's Payne Whitney Gymnasium. Written and directed by Burt Shevelove, with lyrics by Stephen Sondheim, it starred Larry Blyden, Meryl Streep, Christopher Durang and Sigourney Weaver, then students at Yale School of Drama, were in the chorus. *William Baker for Yale Repertory Theatre*

Top left: Playwright August Wilson looks out onto Chapel Street on March 29, 2005, where the Yale Repertory Theatre's kiosk displays a poster for his new — and last — play, "Radio Golf." *Cloe Poisson / Hartford Courant*

Top middle: Meryl Streep, who lives in Salisbury, has been nominated 18 times for an Oscar, winning three, and 28 times for a Golden Globe, winning eight — more nominations than any other actor in the history of either award. Here she rehearses with Joel Brooks at the National Playwrights Conference at the Eugene O'Neill Theater Center in Waterford in 1975. Streep was 26 and had just completed the graduate program at Yale School of Drama. *Eugene O'Neill Theater Center / photograph by A. Vincent Scarano*

Above: Bill Heck, Maggie Lacy and Hallie Foote, the playwright's daughter, perform in the premiere of Horton Foote's landmark "Orphans' Home Cycle," directed by Michael Wilson at Hartford Stage in August 2009. *Rick Hartford / Hartford Courant*

Left: Set designer Alexander Dodge stands in the extraordinary maze of sculpted hedges he created for Hartford Stage's 2013 production of "Twelfth Night," inspired by a suggestion from director Darko Tresnjak. *Cloe Poisson / Hartford Courant*

Connecticut might be the land of steady habits, but it has a soaring literary soul. One could spend a lifetime savoring the works of the writers, playwrights and poets who have called Connecticut home — a pantheon that includes Arthur Miller, William Styron, James Merrill, Philip Roth, Charlotte Perkins Gilman, Ann Petry, Wally Lamb, Madeleine L'Engle and Maurice Sendak, to name a few.

Noah Webster

Famous for his Blue Back Speller and his American dictionary of the English language, Noah Webster was a polymath with strong opinions on politics, conservation, epidemiology, urban planning and education — often expressed in the newspapers of the day.

Having produced the speller, he immediately placed an ad in The Courant to publicize the work and also wrote several articles about the new book that The Courant published.

Webster also penned columns for The Courant in the 1790s, including a series of moralistic essays under the pseudonym "The Prompter" that were so popular they were subsequently published in book form.

In one of the columns, "When a Man is going down hill, everyone gives him a kick," Webster wrote, "While a man is doing very well, that is, while his credit is good, every one helps him — the moment he is pressed for money, however honest and able he may be, he gets kicks from all quarters."

The collected columns in book form sold for decades in 100 editions.

Harriet Beecher Stowe

When Litchfield native Harriet Beecher Stowe wrote "Uncle Tom's Cabin, or Life Among the Lowly," she could not have imagined that for generations it would rack up sales second only to the Holy Bible.

By the standards of her day, though, Stowe pulled her punches. One of the most influential books of its time —

Above: Noah Webster, in an engraving by H.B. Hill based on a painting by Samuel F.B. Morse.
The Connecticut Historical Society

Above: Webster's essay on noses, published on Jan. 10, 1791, under the pseudonym "The Prompter," was one of a series of his often humorous essays The Courant ran in the late 18th century. *Hartford Courant archives*

Right: "Uncle Tom's Cabin" was reprinted by many publishing houses. This paper-wrapped edition published by John C. Jewett and Co. in late 1852 was the least expensive available, selling for 37 1/2 cents.
Harriet Beecher Stowe Center

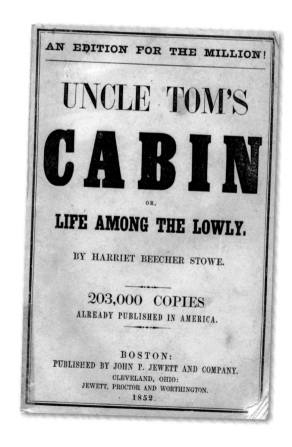

of all time — ends with former slaves leaving the country, a political solution supported in part by Southern slave-owners worried about the presence of too many formerly enslaved people walking around free.

But Stowe wasn't writing a political tract. She was writing an emotional response to slavery. She intended to ignite and excite the general public, and she accomplished what no radical editor, no fiery speeches could do: She forced slavery into the genteel parlors and inatten-tive churches, and once there — for or against — the topic could no longer be denied.

Mark Twain

After moving to Hartford in 1871, Samuel Clemens — already well-known as the writer Mark Twain — soon became The Courant's darling. Throughout the 1870s the newspaper reported the Clemenses' attendance at social events and fundraisers, such as a spelling bee at Asylum Hill Congregational Church in 1875.

"I don't see any use in having a uniform and arbitrary way of spelling words," he was reported as having said at the bee. "We might as well make all clothes alike and cook all dishes alike. Sameness is tiresome; variety is pleasing."

And in May 1875 he bought a famed classified ad after his umbrella was swiped at a baseball game on the South Meadows:

> *TWO HUNDRED & FIVE DOLLARS REWARD — At the great baseball match on Tuesday, while I was engaged in hurrahing, a small boy walked off with an English-made brown silk UMBRELLA belonging to me, & forgot to bring it back. I will pay $5 for the return of that umbrella in good condition to my house on Farmington avenue. I do not want the boy (in an active state) but will pay two hundred dollars for his remains.*
> *– SAMUEL L. CLEMENS.*

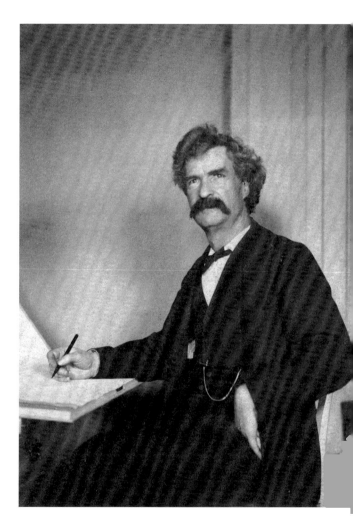

Above: Mark Twain, circa 1881 to 1885.
Mark Twain House and Museum, Hartford

Above: Harriet Beecher Stowe, circa 1869, was an international celebrity when she sat for this portrait taken in Montreal by renowned photographer William Notman, known as "Photographer to the Queen."
Harriet Beecher Stowe Center, Hartford

Wallace Stevens

In the nearly 40 years that poet Wallace Stevens lived in Hartford, he didn't appear to care at all about the lack of attention from the press and often went out of his way to avoid it.

Eventually, his hometown newspaper caught up with him. By then he was 70.

It was 1950, and he had won Yale University's Bollingen Prize for Poetry for his "contribution to American poetry" and the National Book Award. The Courant noted that "in Hartford, he has avoided not only the glare of publicity but any publicity at all."

Edward Parone wrote in The Courant that when Stevens was awarded the Bollingen Prize, "he was almost a stranger in his own home-town." Asked by telephone on the occasion of this honor for an interview, Stevens reportedly said, "I have nothing to say except 'Hooray,'" and hung up.

Parone observed: "It is not that Mr. Stevens, incidentally, has never rhymed before but one does not expect him to rhyme at such a time."

Parone also wrote that Stevens recently had consented to have a new photograph taken by the newspaper: "'Can we come out right away?' asked the reporter. 'Good heavens, no,' was the answer. 'I never wear a clean shirt on a rainy day. Some nice sunny day...' Click!"

Above: Wallace Stevens never learned to drive. He composed his poems as he walked the 2-mile route from his home in Hartford's West End to his office, where he was vice president of the Hartford Accident and Indemnity Co. The route is memorialized with 13 markers that quote his poem "Thirteen Ways Of Looking At A Blackbird." *Nancy Schoeffler / Hartford Courant*

Left: Pulitzer Prize-winning poet Wallace Stevens first wrote under the pseudonym "Peter Parasol."
Sylvia Salmi / Hartford Courant archives

Above: The Irish-American playwright Eugene O'Neill, pictured in 1926, spent his summers at his home in New London. Winner of the Nobel Prize for Literature, O'Neill described his most famous and strongly autobiographical play, "Long Day's Journey Into Night," as having been written "in tears and blood... with deep pity and understanding and forgiveness for all the four haunted Tyrones."
Nickolas Murray / Museum of the City of New York

Wadsworth Atheneum Museum of Art

In its early days, it was not at all clear that the Wadsworth Atheneum Museum of Art would still be around 170 years later.

Old Lyme artist Henry White painted a sorrowful picture of the museum he had visited as a boy in the 1860s and '70s: "The picture gallery was a sepulchral chamber. The dim light filtered down from an opening in the lofty ceiling as into a well. The place had a musty odor. One spoke in whispers, for one's voice echoed with a grim and startling effect."

The Atheneum opened in July 1844, but within a decade, the brainchild of Daniel Wadsworth was sputtering. In 1855 it lowered its admission price from 25 cents to 15 cents, and in the 1880s it closed its galleries for a time. But in the darkest times, angels have come to the rescue — notably J.P. Morgan and Elizabeth Colt.

And no one did a better job of breathing new life into the institution than museum director A. Everett "Chick" Austin. From 1927 to 1944, Austin's impeccable taste and unstoppable energy set the tone for the museum's history ever since.

Austin's avant-garde sensibilities shook up the traditionalist Hartford art establishment. He often clashed with the museum's board about spending and acquisitions that the trustees found excessive and exhibits and events they found mystifying.

But Austin forged ahead, and today his reign is considered the museum's most glorious period, a time when Hartford led the country in its embrace of modern art, inspiring architect Le Corbusier to call Hartford "a spiritual center of America."

Austin filled the museum with Ernst, Klee, Cornell, Calder and countless other cutting-edge artists. He gave Edward Hopper his first one-man museum show, staged the country's first Surrealist exhibit and presented the first-ever retrospective of work by Pablo Picasso in the United States.

He also sponsored the emigration of Russian choreographer George Balanchine, premiering his first American ballet, "Serenade," and staged the world premiere of "Four Saints in Three Acts," an avant-garde opera by Gertrude Stein and Virgil Thomson with an all-black cast playing European saints, which was unprecedented on the American stage. Thomson called Austin "a whole cultural movement in one man."

Below left: An 1847 broadside advertises "upwards of" 100 oil paintings at the Wadsworth Atheneum.
Hartford Courant archives

Below: Chick Austin performs as the Great Osrami in "The Sea God of Magic" at the Wadsworth Atheneum Theatre in 1944.
Ted Kosinski / Wadsworth Atheneum Museum of Art

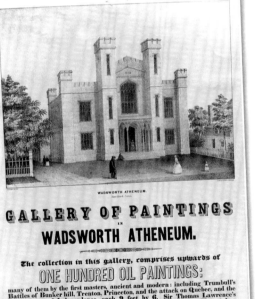

Opposite: "Wall Drawing #1131, Whirls and Twirls (Wadsworth)," a 2004 work by Chester artist Sol LeWitt, electrifies the Morgan Stairs at the Atheneum. LeWitt, who grew up in Hartford, took art classes at the museum as a boy. *Wadsworth Atheneum Museum of Art, Hartford*

Left: Born in 1826 to a prosperous family in Hartford, Frederic Edwin Church was a central figure in the Hudson River School of American landscape painters, known for the romanticism of his luminous scenes. *Brady-Handy Photograph Collection / Wikimedia Commons*

Below right: Florence Griswold owned a boarding house that was the heart of the Lyme Art Colony, which thrived from 1899 to 1937. Connecticut's lovely scenery lured American impressionists including Childe Hassam, Allen Butler Talcott, Henry Ward Ranger, Willard Metcalf, Edward Charles Volkert and Henry Rankin Poore to Lyme. Griswold's home is now the Florence Griswold Museum in Old Lyme. *Florence Griswold Museum*

Below left: Impressionist painters in the "Hot Air Club" sit outdoors for a meal at the height of the Lyme Art Colony days. *Florence Griswold Museum*

New Britain Museum of American Art

John Butler Talcott had no artistic inclination himself. He was an entrepreneur who founded two successful hosiery factories in New Britain. But he understood the value of art in improving people's minds. In 1903, Talcott bequeathed to the fledgling New Britain Institute, an educational community gathering place, money to buy paintings.

That's how the country's first museum dedicated solely to American art came into being.

Today, the New Britain Museum of American Art has 11,000 works of art and occupies an elegant, still-expanding space a few blocks from the original site of the New Britain Institute.

Right below: William Merritt Chase's painting of John Butler Talcott, the museum's founder.
New Britain Museum of American Art

Left: During a 2012 visit to the New Britain Museum of American Art with his grandparents, Timmy Baumer of West Hartford looks up at "The Gravity of Color," Lisa Hoke's colorful plastic and paper cup mosaic.
Patrick Raycraft / Hartford Courant

Above: Theodate Pope, Connecticut's first female architect, designed Hill-Stead, a Colonial revival mansion in Farmington, as a home for her parents, housing their extensive private art collection, and later lived there with her husband. Now the Hill-Stead Museum, it hosts the Sunken Garden Poetry Festival on the grounds in the summer.
Hartford Courant archives

Above: Sculptor Alexander Calder, shown in his workshop at home in Roxbury in 1953, was a pioneer in kinetic art and renowned for inventing the mobile.
Hartford Courant file photo

Below: Schoolchildren from Hartford have lunch beside Alexander Calder's "Stegosaurus" sculpture on Main Street in downtown Hartford in October 1993.
Cecilia Prestamo / Hartford Courant

Classical Music

The notable music figures who either were born in Connecticut or made the state their home — including Marian Anderson, Leroy Anderson, Victor Borge, Paul Hindemith, Moshe Paranov, Paul Robeson, Leonard Bernstein and Rosa Ponselle — suggests the vitality and range of Connecticut's musical history.

But if any one person can be said to be Connecticut's musical patron saint, it is the brilliant, irascible, visionary, perplexing Danbury native Charles Ives, Charlie to his friends. Ives grew up in western Connecticut, imbibing the sounds of marching bands, hymn-singing congregations of various Christian denominations, the standard European classical titans, and the popular songs of the day. In his time, he would incorporate all of those sounds into his compositions, sometimes simultaneously.

Ives' output was not exceptionally large, and most of his oeuvre was composed before he was 50 or so. The music that he did write — including pieces like "Three Places in New England" and "The Holiday Symphony," now considered modern masterpieces — was almost totally ignored during his lifetime. As testimony to Ives' lonely road as a composer, his Third Symphony won a Pulitzer Prize for music in 1947, 38 years after it was written.

Though Ives is now internationally admired as a 20th-century giant, his sudden and surprising dissonances, his odd combinations of instruments and his tendency to start new ideas on a dime still baffle listeners and, not infrequently, performers.

Right: William Mortensen, manager of Bushnell Memorial Hall, greets Marian Anderson, the famous contralto, in this undated photo. Anderson, a Danbury resident, was the first African-American to perform with the Metropolitan Opera. She famously performed at the Lincoln Memorial in Washington on Easter Sunday 1939, after being refused permission to sing at the Daughters of the American Revolution Constitution Hall. *Hartford Courant archives*

Far right: Hartford Symphony Orchestra members John Riley, left, and Jeff Krieger play at a rehearsal in Hartford in October 1982. *Kathy Hanley / Hartford Courant*

Below right: Composer Charles Ives. *Hartford Courant file photo*

Below middle: Karen Hunt, as Mimi, and Michael Talley, as Rodolfo, perform Act III of Giacomo Puccini's "La Boheme" during the dress rehearsal of the Connecticut Opera's 1983 production at Bushnell Memorial Hall. *Michael Lennahan / Hartford Courant*

Below far right: Dr. Moshe Paranov, president emeritus of the Hartt College of Music, plays a number of songs in December 1971 for the Fine Arts Commission, which was searching for an official state song, as the commission's musical consultant, Charles Fidlar, sings the lyrics. The legislature adopted "Yankee Doodle" as the state song in 1978. *John Long / Hartford Courant*

The Jazz Age

In 1926, The Courant polled readers whether the performance of jazz should be permitted in public on Sundays. The convention-flouting music lost by a landslide — with 1,143 readers voting to keep Sunday safe from the corrupting temptations of jazz. Only 349 readers lined up in favor of allowing Satan's latest sinful, musical concoction to profane the Sabbath.

Below left: In the early 1960s, when rock music seemed an irresistible force that threatened to crush jazz, artists like alto saxophonist Jackie McLean helped keep it going. McLean later founded the nationally recognized jazz program at the University of Hartford's Hartt School. *Hartford Courant archives*

Below right: Jazz pianist Dave Brubeck performs May 4, 1989, at the University of Connecticut's Jorgensen Auditorium. *Fred Beckham / Special to The Courant*

But as the Jazz Age evolved and popular culture — everything from silent films, the rising radio craze, flapper fashions, hip flasks and hip music — became an irresistibly powerful social force, the syncopated sounds became increasingly popular in Hartford.

Duke Ellington, who began appearing in Hartford in the 1930s, was one of the major pioneering black artists whose music leaped over the hurdles of the period's steep racist barriers, mesmerizing crossover audiences.

A Woodstock That Wasn't

The Powder Ridge Music Festival, which lured thousands of music fans to Middlefield in late July 1970, was probably doomed from the beginning, with objections from town officials and court rulings blocking the event as the date approached.

In June 1970 The Courant reported that 25 musical acts and 50,000 fans were expected to attend the three-day festival. "It's going to happen much easier than Woodstock," one of the promoters assured the paper.

The planned lineup included Eric Burdon & War, Sly and the Family Stone, Fleetwood Mac, Melanie, Mountain, James Taylor, Joe Cocker, the Allman Brothers, Little Richard, Van Morrison, Jethro Tull, Janis Joplin, Chuck Berry, Grand Funk Railroad, Richie Havens, Ten Years After and more.

But it wasn't to be — with the exception of the folk singer Melanie, who, defying a court-ordered injunction against performers, famously entertained the crowd.

Above: Bruce Springsteen performs with the E Street Band at the Hartford Civic Center in May 2000. *John Woike / Hartford Courant*

Below: John Julian of Colorado strums a guitar as crowds wait for the Powder Ridge Music Festival in Middlefield on July 29, 1970. A court order barring performances halted the festival, but thousands of people showed up anyway. *Arman G. Hatsian / Hartford Courant*

Above: Members of the Pilobolus Dance Theater perform their signature piece "Ciona" at Bushnell Park in Hartford in May 1974, as part of Peace Train's Summerdance series. *Steve Silk / Hartford Courant*

Right: In Hartford Ballet's 1988 production of "The Nutcracker," Chris Lux Rieger, left, and Jane Scichili Martin prepare to move out onto the stage for the "Dance of the Flowers." *John Long / Hartford Courant*

SPIRIT OF COMPETITION

The Courant's readers learned the news on the morning of March 8, 1877, seven weeks before the start of the second National League baseball season: Hartford, a charter member, was deemed unacceptable as a major league market.

The city's "base ball" team, founded by Morgan G. Bulkeley three years earlier, would be moving to Brooklyn, N.Y., and would be known as the "Hartford club of Brooklyn."

The news item said the team would retain the prestige of its old name while "acquiring the prestige which comes from locating in a large city."

So there it was, 120 years before Peter Karmanos uprooted the Whalers from Connecticut's capital city. The state's first audition as a major league sports market was over after one season when the Dark Blues left for New York City.

Thus began Connecticut's sports identity crisis.

Nestled between Boston and New York, the state has been told repeatedly that it does not measure up to its large neighbors as a sports market.

Professional sports franchises in traditional sports (basketball, football) and nontraditional sports (arena football, indoor soccer) have come and gone. Minor league teams have failed, major league teams have flirted with the market, and facility proposals have stalled as political and business leaders struggled to craft a plan, decade after decade.

At the same time, UConn athletics have developed into a national brand that has become a point of passionate pride across Connecticut, and other colleges and universities around the state have enjoyed their own glorious moments.

Is Connecticut a minor-league state? Or has it evolved to thrive in a particular niche as New England's largest college sports market? The questions reach back to the Dark Blues' defection to Brooklyn and the New England Patriots' decision to walk away from Adriaen's Landing, and they still hover over the state today.

Left: UConn women's basketball head coach Geno Auriemma is carried off the court by Moriah Jefferson, Kiah Stokes, Brianna Banks, Kaleena Mosqueda-Lewis and Bria Hartley after the Huskies defeated Notre Dame for the 2014 NCAA Women's National Championship — the UConn women's ninth national title.
John Woike / Hartford Courant

Left: The Hartford Dark Blues, shown in 1875, were owned by Bulkeley, a future Connecticut governor and the first National League president. The team was a member of the National Association of Professional Base Ball Players in 1874 and 1875 before joining the National League as a charter member in 1876. The Hartfords, as they were called in The Courant, played on land leased from Elizabeth Colt, on Wyllys Street next to the Church of Good Shepherd. They were 47-21-6, finishing in third place. But the team was sold and moved to Brooklyn after one season.
Prescott & White, Heritage Auction Gallery, through WikiCommons

Below right: Ed Lenthe, right, a pitcher for the Hartford Chiefs, and teammates watch a game at Bulkeley Stadium in April 1952. *Courant file photo*

Right: At age 51, Babe Ruth, with the last of his 714 home runs a decade behind him, visited Hartford in 1945 for an exhibition game with the Savitt Gems. Ruth, seventh from the left in the back row, stands next to team owner Bill Savitt, in the suit. Cliff Keeney, who provided this photo, is in the bottom row, third from the left. The Courant reported that when emcee and radio personality Bob Steele asked Ruth about hitting, he replied, "Some days the balls look like watermelons, some days like peanuts."
Courtesy of Cliff Keeney

'THE FABULOUS PEP'

Hartford boxer Willie Pep, who started 62-0 before losing his 63rd fight and then went 73 more fights without a loss, fought a remarkable 241 times in his 27-year career, finishing with a record of 229-11-1. Pep won back the world title in a rematch with Sandy Saddler on Feb. 11, 1949, at Madison Square Garden. In the next day's paper The Courant's Bill Lee wrote: "The fabulous Pep became the first undisputed featherweight champion in ring history to regain the throne. Knocked out in 2:38 of the fourth round of his first fight with Saddler last October 29, Pep rallied his forces tonight to give one of the most masterly exhibitions of boxing skill any champion ever made in the Garden ring."

Left and right: Willie Pep.
Courant file photos

Left: Before the rise of greyhounds and jai alai in Connecticut, trotters fed the appetite for gambling. Charter Oak Park in Hartford, shown in this advertisement, drew big crowds and some of the best horses until it closed in the 1930s. "The feeling among horsemen has been one of satisfaction with the accommodation provided for stock, and the treatment they have received personally," The Courant reported in 1874 after a highly successful first year at the race track. *The Connecticut Historical Society*

Above: Walter Camp, pictured during his days as Yale's football captain in 1878-1879, served as Yale football coach for 34 years and is considered to be "the father of college football." Under his leadership, Yale lost only 14 games from 1876 to 1909. *Hartford Courant archives*

Above right: In 1926, Hartford was back in the big leagues when sports promoter George Mulligan's Hartford Blues football team joined the NFL. The Blues played at the East Hartford Velodrome, but the team finished 3-7, and bad weather stifled attendance all season. Mulligan was unable to pay his coaches and players, and the team was dropped from the NFL after one season. *Hartford Courant archives*

THE BLUES LEFT, AND THE PATRIOTS NEVER CAME

On Nov. 19, 1998, the deal was signed: After a decade of flirting, the New England Patriots were moving to Hartford.

"Touchdown!" the front-page head-line gushed in a special street edition of The Courant. The state would build a $374 million stadium in downtown Hartford and the Patriots would relocate in 2001.

Fast forward to April 30, 1999. Patriots owner Robert Kraft spiked the deal, citing construction delays. Massachusetts was sweetening its own deal to keep the team — and the Patriots stayed put.

Opposite: Gov. John G. Rowland signs a memo of intent with Robert Kraft, owner of the New England Patriots, in front of a backdrop of smiling legislators, Hartford Mayor Mike Peters, behind Kraft, and Robert Fiondella, CEO of The Phoenix, far right, at a press conference at the state Capitol on Nov. 19, 1998. Half a year later Kraft nixed the deal. *Cloe Poisson / Hartford Courant*

'BEST OF THE CENTURY' LIST: STILL HOTLY DEBATED

In the summer of 1999 as Y2K approached, a panel of 17 experts sifted through 100 years of Connecticut athletes' accomplishments for The Courant, considering only those athletes who had spent their formative years — when they were shaping their athletic abilities — in the state (so don't look for Jim Calhoun or Geno Auriemma or stars who have emerged in more recent years).

The panelists weighed individual honors, achievements and the influence each athlete had on his or her sport. The Courant compiled each panelist's top 15 votes and then developed a list of the top 25.

Like so much in the world of sports, particularly in a state with such ardent fans, the list remains a matter of lively debate 15 years later.

1. Steve Young: Attended Greenwich High. NFL quarterback and Pro Football Hall of Fame.

2. Calvin Murphy: Born in Norwalk; attended Norwalk High. Basketball Hall of Fame.

3. Willie Pep: Born in Middletown; lived in Hartford and Wethersfield. Boxing Hall of Fame.

4. Joan Joyce: Born in Waterbury; attended Crosby High. Softball Hall of Fame.

5. Bruce Jenner: Attended Newtown High. Olympic decathlon gold medalist.

6. Jeff Bagwell: From Killingworth; attended Xavier High-Middletown and University of Hartford. Baseball All-Star.

7. Andy Robustelli: Born in Stamford; attended Stamford High and

Far left: Bruce Jenner joyfully crosses the finish line as he sets a new world record and wins the gold medal in the decathlon at the 1976 Summer Olympics in Montreal. *Corbis Images*

Left: Kristine Lilly, left, of the USA and Marit Christensen of Norway fight for the ball during the Women's World Cup Send-Off Series at Rentschler Field in East Hartford in July 2007.
Patrick Raycraft / Hartford Courant

Opposite, left: UConn guard Jennifer Rizzotti, who went on to coach for the University of Hartford, fights for control of the ball during UConn's victory in the 1995 Big East Tournament.
Albert Dickson / Hartford Courant

Arnold College in Milford. Pro Football Hall of Fame.

8. Walt Dropo: Born in Moosup; attended Plainfield High and UConn. Three-sport UConn star and professional baseball player.

9. Brian Leetch: Raised in Cheshire; attended Cheshire High and Avon Old Farms. NHL All-Star and Hockey Hall of Fame.

10. Meadowlark Lemon: Lived in Fairfield. Harlem Globetrotter.

11. Floyd Little: Attended Hillhouse High-New Haven. College Football Hall of Fame and Pro Football Hall of Fame.

12. Bobby Valentine: Born in Stamford; attended Rippowam High. Major League Baseball All-Star.

13. Kristine Lilly: Attended Wilton High. Olympic gold medal soccer player.

14. Dorothy Hamill: Raised in Riverside. Olympic gold medal figure skater, U.S. Figure Skating Hall of Fame and U.S. Olympic Hall of Fame.

15. Bill Rodgers: Born in Hartford; attended Newington High and Wesleyan. Multiple marathon winner, including Boston and New York.

16. Ken Strong: Born in West Haven; attended West Haven High. Pro Football Hall of Fame.

17: Lindy Remigino: Attended Hartford Public High. Olympic gold medal sprinter.

18: Vin Baker: Attended Old Saybrook High and University of Hartford. NBA first-round draft pick.

19: Mo Vaughn: Born and raised in Norwalk. Major League Baseball All-Star.

20: Julius Boros: Born in Fairfield; attended Ludlowe High and the University of Bridgeport. 18 PGA Tour victories.

21: Jimmy Piersall: Born in Waterbury; attended Leavenworth High. Major League Baseball All-Star.

22. John Williamson: Attended Wilbur Cross High. ABA champion and NBA player.

23. Jen Rizzotti: Attended New Fairfield High and UConn. College basketball player of the year; coach at University of Hartford.

24. Chris Drury: Raised in Trumbull; attended Fairfield Prep. Little League World Series champion; NHL All-Star.

25. John Egan: Born in Hartford; attended Weaver High. College NIT champion and NBA player.

Above left: Gold medal winner Dorothy Hamill beams during the medal presentation for women's figure skating at the 1976 Olympics in Innsbruck, Austria. *AP/Corbis*

Above right: Bill Rodgers wears a crown of laurels after winning his fourth straight New York City Marathon in October 1979. *Bettmann/Corbis*

Right: Ron Francis, following through after taking a slap shot, is widely regarded as the greatest Whaler. He holds the most offensive records, including goals, assists, points and games.

Richard Mei / Hartford Courant

Left: In 1977, Whalers owner Howard Baldwin outmaneuvered Montreal, Detroit and Boston to bring Gordie Howe and his two sons to Hartford — a hat trick that helped vault the team into the NHL two years later. Gordie Howe, left, and sons Mark, center, and Marty, right, wave as a banner is raised honoring their family in March 2011 at the XL Center in Hartford.

Tia Ann Chapman / Hartford Courant

Above: Peter Karmanos, who bought the Whalers in 1994, promised to keep the team in Hartford for at least four years. By 1997, the beloved Whalers left. Fans were heartbroken. Mike Fitch of Canterbury, left, consoles his friend Dave Dickenson after the last game on April 13, 1997.

Marc Yves Regis I / Hartford Courant

Right: Whalers captain Kevin Dineen, who scored the last goal in Hartford NHL history for a 2-1 win over Tampa Bay, takes the last lap around the ice after the final game.

Tom Brown / Hartford Courant

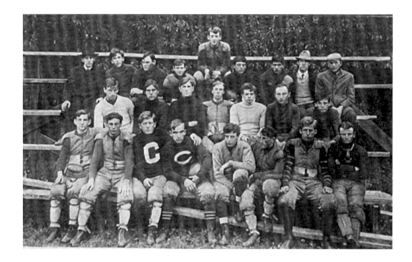

Left: The Connecticut Agricultural College football team in 1906; the college formed its first team in 1896. *University of Connecticut Photograph Collection*

Below left: UConn football head coach Skip Holtz gets the traditional dunking in the final seconds of the team's 28-27 victory over the University of Massachusetts in November 1998. UConn advanced to the Division I-AA playoffs for the first time. *Michael McAndrews / Hartford Courant*

Below right: In 2007, UConn won its first Big East championship but lost in the Meineke Car Care Bowl. Larry Taylor is thrown after catching a screen pass against Wake Forest during the bowl's first half. *John Woike / Hartford Courant*

Left: Richard Hamilton, left, and Khalid El-Amin embrace after UConn's victory over Duke University in the NCAA Champsionship in March 1999 in St. Petersburg, Florida. *Richard Messina / Hartford Courant*

Far left: In 1901, the Connecticut Agricultural College in Storrs fielded a men's basketball team and beat Windham High 17-12 in its first recorded game. The team pictured is from 1903. *University of Connecticut Photograph Collection*

Below: Kemba Walker, a first team All-American as a junior in 2011, led UConn to its third national championship that year by averaging 23.5 points in 41 games. Walker scored 16 points in the championship game against Butler. *Patrick Raycraft / Hartford Courant*

Above: UConn coach Jim Calhoun celebrates the Huskies' 53-41 win over Butler for the NCAA National Tournament championship in Houston in April 2011. Calhoun retired the following year, after 873 wins and three national championships. *Bettina Hansen / Hartford Courant*

Left: Emeka Okafor celebrates UConn's victory over Georgia Tech in San Antonio in April 2004 for its second national championship. *Richard Messina / Hartford Courant*

Above: Shabazz Napier holds up four fingers in the closing seconds of the NCAA Tournament's East Regional final at Madison Square Garden on March 30, 2014. UConn's 60-54 win over Michigan State took the team to the Final Four the following week in Arlington, Texas, where Napier led the Huskies to their fourth national championship title, defeating Kentucky 60-54 on April 7, 2014. Coming off an NCAA Tournament ban and competing in a new conference under second-year coach Kevin Ollie, the team had not been viewed as a contender. *Richard Messina / Hartford Courant*

Top left: In 1902 Connecticut Agricultural College fielded its first women's basketball team. *University of Connecticut Photograph Collection*

Bottom left: Rebecca Lobo anticipates a No. 1 ranking for the first time in the UConn women's basketball team's history after No. 2 UConn defeated No. 1-ranked University of Tennessee 77-66 at Gampel Pavilion on Jan. 16, 1995. UConn went on to beat Tennessee for its first NCAA championship that April, capping a perfect 35-0 season, and Lobo was named MVP of the tournament. *Albert Dickson / Hartford Courant*

Left: Maya Moore, who led UConn to a 150-4 record in four years, including four Final Four appearances and two national titles, floats unchallenged to the basket to score her 2,001st point during the 2010 Big East tournament quarterfinal at the XL Center. She was the first player to reach the 2000-point mark as a junior at UConn and left as its all-time scorer with 3,036 points. *Cloe Poisson / Hartford Courant*

Below Breanna Stewart drives to the hoop during open practice for the 2014 NCAA Women's Final Four, which UConn won — its ninth national title — in Nashville in April 2014. She was named the Final Four's most outstanding player for the second straight season. *John Woike / Hartford Courant*

Above: UConn men's soccer coach Ray Reid watches the action during the first half against Temple University on Oct. 22, 2014, when he got his 400th win. Reid, who has led UConn to 16 consecutive NCAA Tournament appearances, also spent eight seasons at Southern Connecticut State University and has been honored as national coach of the year four times.

John Woike / Hartford Courant

Above left: Bill Detrick spent 29 years as the men's basketball coach at Central Connecticut State University, where the campus gymnasium now bears his name. He later spent 23 years as coach of the Trinity men's golf team before retiring in 2013 at age 86. *Central Connecticut State University*

Above: Vikram Malhotra, Johan Detter, coach Paul Assaiante and Parth Sharma celebrate the Trinity men's squash team's 13th consecutive national championship in February 2011, besting Yale in their closest match that season. The team won 252 matches in a row, a streak spanning nearly 14 years, before losing to Yale the following year; the team then rebounded to win its 14th title in 2013. *Shawn Courchesne / Hartford Courant*

Above right: Joe Morrone, who led the Huskies to their first NCAA championship in 1981, is pictured that year talking with Eric Myren. Hired as the UConn men's soccer coach in 1969, Morrone went on to coach for 28 seasons, and when he retired the university named the soccer stadium on campus after him. *Jerry Williams / Hartford Courant*

Right: Yale football coach Carm Cozza, pictured in 1989, retired in 1996 after 32 years with Yale. He led the Bulldogs to 10 Ivy League championships. *Cloe Poisson / Hartford Courant*

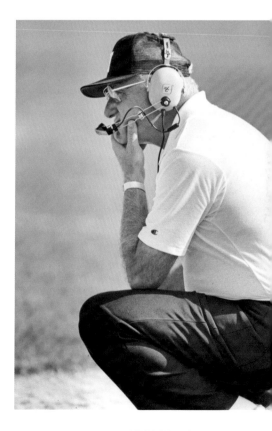

Right: Members of the 2003 Coventry High School volleyball team surround head coach Matt Hurlock after winning their first state title in 10 years. Pictured with Hurlock are, starting at 1 o'clock, Emma Sousa, Tiffany Lathrop, Lori Sereno, Ashley Bergeron, Brittney Conant, Nicole Mills, Samantha Yanez and Kelly Sommariva. Coventry began its volleyball dominance that year, leading to a four-year, 84-match winning streak that Southington broke in 2009, and a 76-match streak that ended with a loss to Granby. In the meantime, Coventry won nine state titles.

John Woike / Hartford Courant

Below: The Cheshire High School girls' swim team celebrates its victory over Branford in October 2007, when it broke the national record for the longest dual meet streak in the country. Cheshire didn't lose for another four years, when Glastonbury beat the Rams, ending what was then a 25-year streak.

John Woike / Hartford Courant

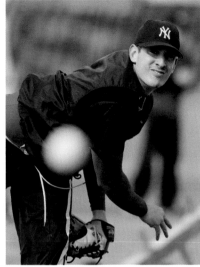

Left: As a senior at Fitch High School in Groton in 2007, Matt Harvey was 6-1 and struck out a school record 112 in 54 2/3 innings. He is now a starting pitcher for the New York Mets. *Michael Kodas / Hartford Courant*

Above: Arkeel Newsome, who now plays for UConn, led Ansonia to three state football titles. He set the 2013 state season rushing record with 3,867 yards and the state career rushing record with 10,672. *Brad Horrigan / Hartford Courant*

Right: Joe Grippo, who has coached girls volleyball at Morgan High School in Clinton for three decades, winning 12 state titles for Morgan and a spot in the Connecticut Women's Volleyball Hall of Fame, gets his team pumped up between sets while playing against Coginchaug High School in Durham in October 2013. *Stephen Dunn / Hartford Courant*

Above: Billy Casper celebrates his victory in the 1965 Insurance City Open, the second of his four wins in Connecticut. *Maurice Murray / Hartford Courant*

Right: Arnold Palmer later won plenty of PGA tournaments, but he won his first PGA event in the United States in Connecticut at the 1956 Insurance City Open. He made a birdie at the par-5 second playoff hole to defeat Ted Kroll. *Courant archives*

Above: Fan favorite Bubba Watson is moved to tears after winning the 2010 Travelers, his first PGA Tour victory. *John Woike / Hartford Courant*

Left: Amateur Bill Whedon of West Hartford, who played in the 1955 Insurance City Open, is believed to be the first of only two players in PGA Tour history to record two holes-in-one in the same round in a professional tour event. He aced Nos. 5 and 9 in the first round on Sept. 2, 1955, at the Wethersfield Country Club. The odds of a golfer's doing that in the same round are reportedly one in 67 million. *John Woike / Hartford Courant*

Opposite: Boats from a race of men's college eights collect under the Founders Bridge in Hartford, after crossing the finish line during the 11th Annual Head of the Riverfront Rowing Regatta in October 2009. *Tia Ann Chapman / Hartford Courant*

YANKEE INGENUITY

Mark Twain nailed the description of a Connecticut Yankee innovator.

The year was 1889, less than a decade after Twain had produced what likely was the first book manuscript written on a typewriter. Hartford was a dynamic manufacturing center, with the great factories, forges and machine-makers of the age supplying the world with typewriters, bicycles, clocks, sewing machines, steam engines and newer, faster guns.

Two former Colt Armory mechanics named Francis Pratt and Amos Whitney had defined the inch down to the nearest few millionths — and in so doing invented precision manufacturing. Bicycle-maker Albert Pope, on whose contraption Twain loved to tool around town, would become the most important car manufacturer in the nation within a dozen years.

This was the setting that nurtured Twain's time-traveling character in his satirical "A Connecticut Yankee in King Arthur's Court."

"I am an American. I was born and reared in Hartford, in the State of Connecticut — anyway, just over the river, in the country. So I am a Yankee of the Yankees — and practical; yes, and nearly barren of sentiment, I suppose — or poetry, in other words. My father was a blacksmith, my uncle was a horse doctor, and I was both, along at first. Then I went over to the great arms factory and learned my real trade; learned all there was to it; learned to make everything: guns, revolvers, cannon, boilers, engines, all sorts of labor-saving machinery. Why, I could make anything a body wanted — anything in the world, it didn't make any difference what; and if there wasn't any quick new-fangled way to make a thing, I could invent one — and do it as easy as rolling off a log."

Twain's era actually was not the high point of Connecticut's drive to innovate; that would come decades later in the age of aviation.

And the culture of ingenuity and forward thinking that gave rise to that drive took root in Connecticut nearly 250 years before Twain described the consummate Yankee.

Left: Colt's Patent Arms Manufacturing Co. workers line up for a photo outside the armory, with its Russian-style onion dome visible in the background, in 1876. The Gatling Gun and Baxter steam engine in the photo are two products the company sent to the U.S. Centennial Exposition in Philadelphia that year.
Connecticut State Library

Above: John Winthrop The Younger, son of the Massachusetts Bay Colony's founding governor, founded New London in 1646 and sought to establish an alchemy research center there to find medical cures. He also was an advocate of iron mining, having co-founded one of the first iron ore mines in the colonies, and later served as governor of Connecticut for nearly 20 years.
Detail of an engraving by Amos Doolittle / Yale University Gallery of Art

Above right: Connecticut's most important iron mines started in Salisbury in 1734, but it wasn't until 1762 that Ethan Allen, then 24, built the area's first blast furnace in Lakeville. Connecticut's cannon industry took off. The furnaces and mills at Allen's foundry in Salisbury created about 880 Revolutionary War cannons. *The Connecticut Historical Society*

Right: This four-pounder cannon was cast in Salisbury and buried in Danbury in 1777 to save it from the British. It was buried and recovered at least three more times before being presented to the Winchester Historical Society in 1914.
John Woike / Hartford Courant

Left: New Haven native Charles Goodyear, in this portrait by George Peter Alexander Healy, endured debtors prison and poverty and repeatedly uprooted his family in his obsessive quest to figure out how to stabilize rubber. *Library of Congress*

Right: In 1796, Amelia Simmons published "American Cookery," the first cookbook in the United States. It included recipes for soft gingerbread, roast turkey with cranberry sauce, Indian pudding and spruce beer. She was the first to use the words "cookie" and "slaw" in print. *The Connecticut Historical Society*

Above: In 1767, Seth Dexter started C. H. Dexter & Sons, a saw and grist mill in Windsor Locks that later made paper and developed new types of products, including the first tissue paper. *Thomas J. Dodd Research Center, University of Connecticut Libraries*

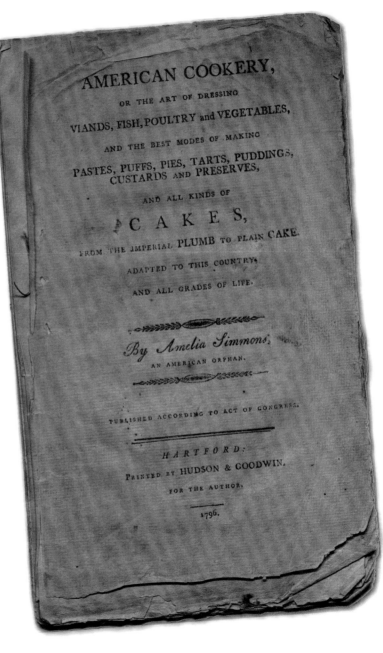

INTERCHANGEABLE PARTS

I n the 21st century, we take it for granted that the parts assembled into manufactured goods are identical — no variations. Making that happen 200 years ago in central Connecticut was a huge advance, the first big step away from handcrafted artisanship toward mass production.

Connecticut had two rising industries, clocks and guns, both making products from small, complex parts, both ripe for revolution.

Yale graduate Eli Whitney's invention of the cotton gin changed the economy of the South but failed as a New Haven business, amid patent disputes and a fire. So in 1798, Whitney used his Yale connections, chiefly with Oliver Wolcott Jr. of Granby, the U.S. Treasury secretary, to win a contract to make 10,000 muskets — something he had never made at all, let alone in huge quantity. He got a cash advance and set up an armory in Hamden.

In an 1801 demonstration for an audience that included President John Adams and President-elect Thomas Jefferson, Whitney talked about making musket parts out of stamping tools and machines that he had devised. (He actually hadn't done so, though. He told his workers to make sure he had a handful of guns with parts that did fit together, for the demonstration.)

One of the people listening was his acquaintance Eli Terry, a clockmaker from East Windsor who had set up shop in Plymouth, now Thomaston. By 1806, Terry inked a deal to sell 4,000 clock mechanisms at a time when a master clockmaker could turn out a few dozen a year.

Terry went on to patent the shelf clock and later sold his enterprise to Seth Thomas and Silas Hoadley, who deployed the burgeoning Waterbury brass industry to make standardized metal workings.

In 1799, Simeon North started making guns at his saw mill, also with the idea of using interchangeable parts. Standardization in the gun trade required not just a new product but a new industry to create it. Like Whitney, North developed equipment, including a milling machine, crucial to forming metal parts without having to file them by hand. His factory in Berlin had the first U.S. contract for pistols and was the first to successfully mass-produce firearms with interchangeable parts.

Above: Eli Whitney, in a portrait by Samuel Finley Breese. *Yale University Art Gallery*

Right: Eli Terry was a clockmaker who set up shop in what is now Thomaston. *The Connecticut Historical Society*

Far right: Clockworks from a timepiece made by Eli Terry. *The Connecticut Historical Society*

THE GREAT MACHINE AGE

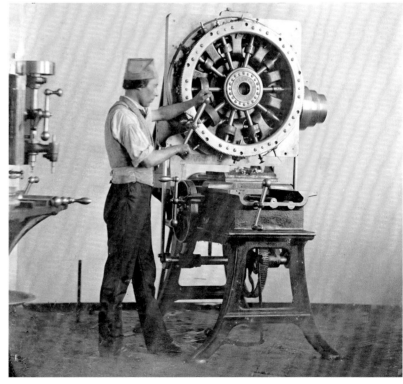

Gun-maker Sam Colt understood a crucial point: Now that interchangeable parts were part of the landscape for clocks, guns and other goods, the next level of progress required an interwoven system of businesses feeding off each other, to build not just products but a modern industrial economy.

It was that industrial ecosystem that built up around Hartford and the rest of the Northeast during Colt's life — not just guns and factory machines and forges, but also hardware, textiles, sewing machines, clocks, evolving forms of insurance and public health systems — that cradled an amazing age of innovation in the mid-19th century.

Guns would still dominate in Connecticut in 1873, a decade after Sam Colt died, as Colt's produced the single-action Army "Peacemaker," and Winchester introduced its Model 1873 rifle. Both firearms would become known as "The Gun That Won the West."

Hartford was established as the machining capital of the world. The stage was set for explosive growth. But that growth would come from products few people at the time had ever seen.

Above: Samuel Colt was born in Hartford in 1814 and died in 1862. His pistol with a revolving cylinder is perhaps the greatest single innovation in firearms history. *Library of Congress*

Above right: The single-action Army .45-caliber revolver was produced by Colt's Patent Firearms Manufacturing Co. in Hartford. *Courant archives*

Below right: A revolver frame jigging machine designed and patented by Samuel Colt. *Connecticut State Library*

RESHAPING DAILY LIFE

Three new inventions had a big debut at the Philadelphia Centennial Exposition in 1876. None was sparked in Connecticut, but all three would drive innovation and the rise of mighty corporations in the state for years to come.

And all three would change the daily lives of thousands of people in the era when technology and democracy finally came together.

The bicycle. The telephone. The typewriter.

Left: An advertisement for Columbia bicycles, made by Albert Pope's Pope Manufacturing Co. on Capitol Avenue in Hartford. Pope, who started the company in 1878, eventually dominated the market. He continually worked to improve the product, making it more lightweight, less expensive and safer, even for women in long skirts. *The Connecticut Historical Society*

Below: Three women in black dresses and white aprons stand at the switchboard at Southern New England Telephone Co. on Main Street and Central Row in Hartford in 1883. The nation's first commercial telephone exchange, it was started several years earlier by George Coy, a former New Haven telegraph manager. Coy had assisted Alexander Graham Bell in a demonstration of telephone technology in 1877, when Bell spoke from a hall in New Haven and an orchestra played in Hartford. He promptly signed on as Bell's local agent. *The Connecticut Historical Society*

Above: A woman sits at an Underwood typewriter, circa 1918. Underwood and its main rival, Royal, competed in Hartford as a new office culture took hold in the latter decades of the 19th century. The insurance industry soon became the largest customer base for typewriters. *Library of Congress*

Opposite: Workers at the Cheney Silk Mills in south Manchester in 1924. *Lewis Hine / Library of Congress*

Far left: Even though it was not on a main trade route, New Britain — with companies like The Stanley Works, Landers Frary & Clark, the Corbin Car Co. — came to be known as the Hardware Capital. Here, a worker examines a product at Fafnir Bearing, which dominated the ball bearing industry for decades. *Library of Congress*

Left: William Boeing, left, visits Pratt & Whitney in Hartford in March 1927 to take a look at the company's Wasp engine. At right is Frederick Rentschler, founder of Pratt & Whitney. *United Technologies Corp., Pratt & Whitney*

Below: An early price list shows the original Bolt Manufactory of Frederick T. Stanley, later Stanley Works, in New Britain. The small one-story wooden building served as an armory in the militia days of 1812. *Courant archives*

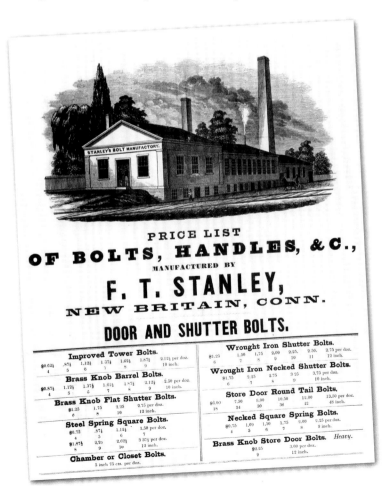

Above: Gustave Whitehead with his No. 21 craft, in 1901. Historians are divided over whether Whitehead flew a powered airplane two years before the Wright brothers.
William O'Dwyer Collection, Fairfield Museum and History Center

Above: Igor Sikorsky flies an early prototype of the VS-300 helicopter. That model's first flight, 3 feet off the ground, came in 1939. *Sikorsky Aircraft Corp.*

Above left: Igor Sikorsky achieved early success in his native Russia building large airplanes before and during World War I, including the first multi-engine bomber. In Connecticut he developed a helicopter with a single rotor. *San Diego Air & Space Museum*

Left: Workers at the Vought-Sikorsky Aircraft Corp. in Stratford in 1940. *Library of Congress*

Top right: In 1955, Trinity College chemistry professor Vernon Krieble and his son Robert, a GE chemist, figured out a way to turn a GE product into an industrial adhesive that cured only in the absence of oxygen. They launched American Sealants, later Loctite, as a revolutionary way for machine companies to lock screws tightly in place at the factory, thereby reducing vibration and enabling microscopic tolerances. *Courant file photo*

Bottom right: H. Joseph Gerber, president of Gerber Scientific, center, looks on with Robert Maerz, president of Gerber Scientific Instrument Co., as systems engineer Mary Ann Deuerling demonstrates a new film preparation system for graphic artists in March 1984. After fleeing Nazi-controlled Austria in 1940 with his mother and settling in Hartford, Gerber used the elastic in his pajamas to invent a device that became the variable scale, the first of a lifetime of devices, including numerically controlled machine tools, that brought him 650 patents. *Stephen Dunn / Hartford Courant*

Far right: Biomedical engineer Eric Sirois is CEO of the startup company Dura Biotech, which has developed a novel replacement heart valve that is inserted using a catheter and is 40 percent smaller than valves now in use. *University of Connecticut*

STILL INNOVATING

As technology today grows in many directions, big corporations such as United Technologies, Pfizer and the insurance companies drive many of the technological advances in Connecticut.

Universities are also driving the breakthroughs, particularly as progress today tends to come from cutting-edge science, rather than the mass production of bright ideas.

For centuries, Connecticut has been a place where those bright ideas have sparked. It's also been a place for the patient, sometimes tedious work of product development, through years of innovating how things are made — sometimes with tiny improvements that make a huge difference.

Below: Guests gather at The Jackson Laboratory before the official opening of the research facility at the University of Connecticut Health Center in Farmington on Oct. 7, 2014.

Michael McAndrews / Hartford Courant

CONNECTICUT HISTORICAL SOCIETY

The Connecticut Historical Society is the official state historical society of Connecticut and one of the oldest historical societies in the nation.

Located at 1 Elizabeth Street in Hartford, CHS houses a private, nonprofit museum, library, archive and education center that is open to the public. The CHS campus houses a research center containing over 3.5 million manuscripts, graphics, books, artifacts, and other historical materials.

In 1825, the Connecticut General Assembly approved the creation of the Connecticut Historical Society to collect objects related to the history of the United States, specifically Connecticut.

With the rise in prominence of Hartford in the 1820s, the Society's committee decided to house its first meetings in the city. The first official quarters for the CHS were over a store at 124 Main Street in Hartford. The CHS began to enroll members from around the state, publish a history and genealogy magazine, and retrieve speakers for lectures who could address groups throughout Connecticut.

With its growing collection of books, pamphlets and objects, the CHS moved its home to a room in the newly built Wadsworth Atheneum in 1843. By 1844, The Society's collection grew to 6,000 pamphlets, 250 bound volumes of newspapers, manuscripts, coins, portraits, and furniture.

To accommodate the growth, the CHS purchased the house of inventor Curtis Veeder at Elizabeth Street in the West End of Hartford in 1950. Alterations to the building in the 1950s-1970s included the addition of book stacks, auditorium, exhibition galleries and reading room.

Connecticut Historical Society
museum & library
1 Elizabeth Street | Hartford, CT 06105
www.chs.org

BIG Y

At Big Y, our goal is to exceed our customers' evolving expectations by constantly seeking better ways to create and deliver World Class service and value.

Headquartered in Springfield, MA, Big Y is one of the largest independently owned supermarket chains in New England. Proud to be family owned and operated, we currently have 61 stores throughout Connecticut and Massachusetts.

At 30 years old, Paul D'Amour was a bread route salesman for the Wonder Bread Baking Company. In 1936, full of entrepreneurial spirit, Paul and his brother Gerry, purchased the *Y Cash Market* in the Wilimansett section of Chicopee, Massachusetts at the intersection where two roads converge to form a "Y". On December 12, 1936, Paul and his brother Gerry began their legacy.

In 1947, the business was incorporated, and the Big Y® Foods, Inc. was born. The brothers opened a second, larger Y Cash Market and continued to grow from there, providing more variety, self service and convenient one-stop shopping. Through the years, much has changed, but what remains the same is our family owned, family oriented focus. Customer service has been and always will be our cornerstone which is why we train all of our more than 10,000 employees with emphasis on just that.

We're proud to be a part of our Massachusetts and Connecticut communities for over 78 years. As the neighborhoods have changed and grown, we have evolved to meet their needs. At Big Y, we're still all about family and community and customer service.

www.bigy.com

P.C. RICHARD & SON

P.C. Richard & Son began as a small hardware store in Bensonhurst, Brooklyn in 1909, founded by Dutch immigrant, Peter Christian Richard. It was transformed by his son, A.J., and later his son Gary Richard, into what is now America's #1 family owned appliance, electronics and mattress retailer with 66 showrooms serving New York, New Jersey, Connecticut and Pennsylvania.

Headquartered in Farmingdale, LI, NY, where PC Richard & Son has its central distribution center, the company has over 1 million square feet of warehousing in NY, NJ & CT, plus 3 owned and operated state-of-the-art service facilities for repairs on appliances to electronics. In Bridgeport, CT, P.C. Richard & Son operates a 70,000 square foot distribution/training/service center that services Connecticut/Massachusetts.

Customers can find the largest selection at the guaranteed lowest prices on a wide variety of exciting products at P.C. Richard & Son, from major appliances, consumer electronics, and mattresses.

All of P.C. Richard & Son's 2,767 employees are dedicated to providing Superior Service Before, During and After the Sale, and giving customers a wonderful and rewarding shopping experience. It starts with friendly and knowledgeable salespeople, who explain all the features of today's high-tech products, by providing next day delivery, as well as offering professional installation and a repair service by company-owned crews.

The company is currently run by the 5th generation of the Richard family and is built on a 105-year tradition...Richard IS Reliable. "In 2009 we opened our first store in Norwalk and today we have a total of seven in Connecticut. P.C. Richard & Son is built on a tradition of taking care of every customer before, during and after the sale and we are very proud to bring this tradition to the state of Connecticut. I am 4th generation and personally want to thank all our customers in Connecticut for a warm welcome and their continued patronage," said Gregg Richard, President & CEO of P.C. Richard & Son.

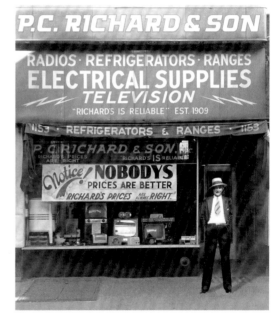

"THE APPLIANCE • TV • ELECTRONICS • MATTRESS GIANT!"

HARTFORD HOSPITAL

Hartford Hospital was born in the wake of an industrial disaster – the 1854 explosion at a Hartford railroad car factory that killed 19 and injured 23 workers. There was no central place to care for the injured. In response, community leaders came together to found Hartford Hospital.

Today, Hartford Hospital is the region's only Level I trauma center, offering the most advanced level of care for the injured, and is the home of LifeStar, the state's first critical-care air medical transport service. A leader in emergency-response best practices, the hospital is one of the founding partners of the Hartford Consensus, which provides recommendations to improve mass-casualty event protocols, designed by national leaders that met on campus. Hartford Hospital was the first hospital in the nation to implement the new standards. With a generous donation from the Hartford Hospital Auxiliary, the hospital installed special bleeding control bags across campus – demonstrating its readiness to respond to any disaster.

In a tough time for health care, Hartford Hospital looks to the future with strength and confidence. In addition to breaking ground on the hospital's world-class Bone & Joint Institute in 2014, the campus will undergo a major expansion of the Center for Education, Simulation & Innovation, which has become a global hub for advanced medical training and health-technology partnerships. This growth continues to advance the hospital's commitment to providing the best care at the best cost to create healthier towns and cities.

Hartford
Hospital
A Hartford HealthCare Partner
80 Seymour Street | Hartford, CT 06102

LUX BOND & GREEN

For over a century, the Lux Bond & Green family has had a singular vision to offer the world's most exquisite diamonds, jewelry, watches and gifts in a comfortable atmosphere with the most knowledgeable professionals in their industry.

From those earliest days in 1898 to today, Lux Bond & Green has grown to seven New England locations with a sound business philosophy: provide exceptional services, distinctive designs, quality products and great values to earn life-long customers.

They have partnered with the most respected international brands such as Rolex, Patek Philippe, David Yurman, Roberto Coin, Marco Bicego, Mikimoto and Simon Pearce.

Compassion is also at the heart of the Green family as demonstrated by the numerous awards they have received for giving back to their communities. Awards from Jewelers for Children, CBIA, UCONN and many others are just some of the recognition Lux Bond & Green has received for their numerous donations. They are also proud to be the Official Jeweler of the Boston Red Sox and the trophy maker to the PGA Travelers Championship and the Manchester Road Race.

Generation after generation has relied on Lux Bond & Green for magnificent gifts that create memories to last a lifetime. It's their attention to every detail that makes the experience truly enjoyable year after year.

The Lux Bond & Green family values its personal relationships with their customers by exceeding their expectations. Each and every visit is important whether it is at their stores, on the phone or visiting their website and faithfully ensuring that EVERY BOX HAS A STORY™.

LUX BOND & GREEN
JEWELRY WATCHES GIFTS • SINCE 1898

West Hartford Center | Glastonbury | Mohegan Sun
Greenwich | Westport | Boston | Wellesley

800.524.7336 | LBGREEN.com

ESTABLISHED 2009

CONNECTICUT SCIENCE CENTER

The Connecticut Science Center is one of the state's newest and most exciting attractions, offering family fun, hands-on science, and educational experiences to visitors from Connecticut and beyond. Since opening in 2009, the Science Center has become an iconic addition to Hartford's skyline and helped reinforce Connecticut's place as a leader in innovation and inspiration.

Located in downtown Hartford, the LEED-Gold certified Connecticut Science Center is dedicated to inspiring lifelong learning through interactive and innovative experiences that explore our changing world through science. Serving 1.8 million people since opening, the Science Center

features more than 165 exhibits that explore such diverse topics as space, earth science, physical science, biology, the Connecticut River watershed, alternative energy, Connecticut inventors and innovations, and much more. Other features include four educational labs, a 200-seat 3D theater, a function room, a gift shop, and events for all ages.

The Connecticut Science Center is home to the Joyce D. and Andrew J. Mandell Academy for Teachers, providing powerful professional development that supports the most current STEM (science, technology, engineering, and mathematics) and curriculum needs. These programs transform classroom instruction,

resulting in engaging learning experiences that lead to achievement for all students.

With international competition for STEM talent, as well as demand for schools to meet challenging new standards, the non-profit Connecticut Science Center inspires learners of all ages to compete in the global marketplace for technology and innovation, helping to create a Connecticut workforce that meets the projected growth of jobs in the STEM fields.

Connecticut Science Center ®

250 Columbus Boulevard | Hartford, CT 06103
CTScienceCenter.org

ESTABLISHED 1988

ADAMS & KNIGHT, INC.

Big ideas that spark measurable growth. That's what Adams & Knight is really in the business of creating for its clients. For more than 25 years, this integrated branding agency has been helping businesses and nonprofits leverage better marketing to achieve bigger goals.

Through its disciplined SparkStorm process, the agency helps organizations hone an engaging and motivating brand positioning – that magic intersection between what they want to say and what their prospects want to hear.

From this cohesive brand platform, the agency then helps clients bring their brand to life across all touchpoints. From traditional advertising and digital marketing to social media and PR, Adams & Knight ensures everything works better by ensuring it all works together to deliver measurable results.

Adams & Knight specializes in working with brands that help others live healthier, wealthier, happier lives. From its Avon, Connecticut headquarters, it serves a wide range of regional, national and global leaders in the health care, financial services and leisure/hospitality sectors.

While the tools in the marketing toolbox have definitely evolved over the last quarter of a century, the "big idea" is still key to success. In fact, the only way to truly stand out in today's crowded marketplace is to stand for something.

And identifying and communicating that brand distinction is exactly what Adams & Knight excels at doing for its clients.

ideas that spark results®
Advertising / Digital Marketing / Social Media / PR
80 Avon Meadow Lane, Avon, CT 06001
860.676.2300 | adamsknight.com

CONNECTICUT AIRPORT AUTHORITY

The Connecticut Airport Authority (CAA) was established as a quasi-public agency in 2011 to own, improve, and operate Bradley International Airport and the five state-owned general aviation airports (Danielson, Groton-New London, Hartford-Brainard, Waterbury-Oxford, and Windham). The CAA strives to provide excellent customer service and top-quality facilities for its passengers while making Connecticut's airports more attractive to new airlines, establishing new routes, and supporting Connecticut's overall economic development and growth strategy.

Originally opened by the federal government as a military air base in 1941, "Bradley Field" was transferred to state control in the mid-1940's and began establishing itself as a major regional resource. Now, Bradley International Airport is the second-largest airport in New England with a customer base that covers the entire Northeast. According to the most recent economic impact analysis, Bradley International Airport contributes $4 billion in economic activity to the state of Connecticut and the surrounding region, representing $1.2 billion in wages and 18,000 full-time jobs.

The CAA's five general aviation airports are also crucial components of the state's overall transportation system, providing access to corporate aircraft, local pilots, and convenient charter service for regional businesses.

Already, the CAA has achieved numerous milestones, including the addition of new Bradley service to Fort Myers, Houston, Tampa, and Washington, D.C. These new routes, and the help of a dedicated passenger base, made Bradley the fastest growing major airport in the region in 2014.

Whether you are traveling to your important business conference or looking for new adventures to explore, the Connecticut Airport Authority is working hard to bring you safe, convenient, and top-quality access to the skies.

CONNECTICUT AIRPORT AUTHORITY

www.ctairports.org
860-292-2000

BRADLEY
INTERNATIONAL

www.bradleyairport.com
860-292-2000

Connecticut Tourism

J ust as it has for centuries, Connecticut remains a haven for original ideas and fresh thinking. A magnet for dreamers and doers, our state offers a dynamic blend of complementary contrasts — a mix of both historic and contemporary attractions, natural and cultural activities, relaxing and active opportunities.

Better still, this diverse blend includes experiences that can be found within easy traveling distance of one another. The state itself spans only about 100 miles from east to west. So in just a few hours time, you can travel from our historic Mystic Country and

scenic southern coastline to the wooded vistas of our northwestern Litchfield Hills. You can go from the quaint small towns of our eastern Quiet Corner to such vibrant westward cities as Hartford, New Haven and Stamford. And all along the way, you can sample everything from romantic B&Bs to modern resorts, from roadside diners to world-class restaurants.

Thanks to the proximity of these varied attractions, both residents and visitors alike find that here in Connecticut, you can travel less — yet experience more. You can escape to the country — while never being far from civilization. And you can go back in time — or

fast-forward into the future.

The DECD Connecticut Office of Tourism invites all those who share our still revolutionary spirit to blaze their own trails and create their own richly varied experiences here in Connecticut.

Simply visit CTvisit.com to learn more about all there is to do — all so close to you.

Connecticut®
still revolutionary
DECD Connecticut Office of Tourism
One Constitution Plaza | Hartford, CT 06103
www.CTvisit.com

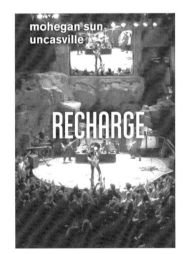

thimble islands stony creek — UNPLUG

mohegan sun uncasville — RECHARGE

mystic seaport mystic — REWIND

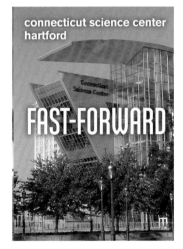

connecticut science center hartford — FAST-FORWARD

SAINT FRANCIS *CARE*

Amazing outcomes. Every day. Saint Francis Hospital and Medical Center has come a long way since 1897, when the Sisters of Saint Joseph of Chambéry overcame near-impossible odds to open a two-room hospital in Hartford's Asylum Hill neighborhood. The new Hospital offered a refuge for immigrants who wanted to know that their faith and traditions would be understood and appreciated if they ever needed care.

From the beginning, Saint Francis served on the front lines against outbreaks of then-deadly infectious diseases, from typhoid fever to influenza, and later polio. At the same time, Saint Francis doctors recognized early that improving health required more than bedside work, and the first research laboratory opened in 1902, the same year that tuberculosis was reaching epidemic proportions in Hartford and across the United States.

While better sanitation, vaccines and antibiotics have tamed many of the early killers, Saint

Francis is even busier today, tackling the healthcare challenges of the modern world with leading-edge technology and treatments. But the very tenets upon which the Hospital was founded – clinical excellence coupled with compassionate caring – have never changed.

From a fledgling hospital with 32 patients in a ward, Saint Francis has grown into an integrated, people-centered healthcare delivery system, the largest independent Catholic healthcare provider in New England, where amazing outcomes take place every day.

SAINT FRANCIS *Care*

114 Woodland Street | Hartford, CT 06105

A

Acquin, Lorne, 126
actors and stage settings, 148, 149–51
Adams & Knight, Avon, 200
agriculture, 29, 34, 35, 42
aircraft, 24, 190, 191
Allen, Ethan, 184
"American Cookery" (Simmons), 185
American Revolution, 67, 68, 69
Anderson, Marian, 160
Andersonville, Georgia, 71
Andrews, Franklin R., 124
Ansonia High School, 179
Anthony, Susan B., on bicycles, 17
anthrax poisoning, Lundgren's death from, 130
Anti-Slavery Almanac, 92
antiwar demonstration, 75
Archer-Gilligan, Amy, 124
Archer Home for Elderly and Indigent Persons, Windsor, 124
architecture, 29, 36–38
Arrigoni Bridge, Middletown, 39
"Arsenal of Democracy" in Civil War, 67
"Arsenic and Old Lace" (Kesselring), 124
arts, 146–63
    about, 147
    actors and stage settings, 148, 149–51
    Bushnell Memorial Hall, 146–47
    dance, 62, 63, 162–63
    Goodspeed Opera House, 149
    literature, 151, 152–54
    music, 49, 149, 160, 161
    New Britain Museum of American Art, 158–59
    painters, 156–57
    Wadsworth Atheneum Museum of Art, 11, 155–57
Asough, Lillian, 97
Assaiante, Paul, 177
Atwater, Dorence, 71
Auriemma, Geno, 164–65
Austin, A. Everett "Chick," 155
automobiles
    1920s, 4–5, 24, 43
    1930s–1950s, 26, 111, 113
    license plates, 43
    major accident, 142
    Pope-Hartford police patrol van, 16
aviation, 24, 183, 190, 191
Avon, 41, 59, 200

B

Baez, Jose, 55
Bagwell, Jeff, 170
Baker, Vin, 171
Balanchine, George, 155, 162
Baldwin, Howard, 172
Banks, Brianna, 164–65
baseball, 166, 179
basketball, 164–65, 171, 174-177
Batterson, James, 38
Batterson, Walter E., *front cover*
Battle of Gettysburg, 70, 71
"Battle of the Marianas" (Kiely), 72
Battles, Richard A., Jr., 100
Baumer, Timmy, 159
Baxter's Painting and Decorating Store, 24
Bechard, Viola, *front cover,* 113
Beck, Matthew, 130
Bendezu, John, 62
Bennett, Jacque, 102
Bergeron, Ashley, 178
Berlin High School, 65
Beth Sholom Synagogue dedication, 54
bicycles
    about, 16, 188
    building a custom wheel for, 60
    Hartford Ladies Cycle Club, 17
    high-wheel bicycles in parade, 16
    police escort for Roosevelt, 43
Big Y World Class Market, 195
Bigos, Barbara, 85
Billipp, Andy, 34
Billipp, Haley Fox, 34
Bishop, Rebecca, 32
Bissell, Daniel, 69
"Black Law," 94
Black Panthers, 101
blizzards/snow storms, 104–5, 106, 107, 116, *back cover*
Block, Adriaen, 7
Bloomfield United Methodist Church "Living Creche," 57
Blum, Rick, 56
Blumenthal, Richard, 131

C

Blyden, Larry, 150
"Boat Building," Phoenix Company, 37
Boeing, William, 190
Bogue Farms, Higganum, 35
Bollingen Prize for Poetry, 154
Bolt Manufactory, New Britain, 190
"Boomerang!" shot in Stamford, 149
Booth, Devin "Moe," 31
Boros, Julius, 171
Bosso, David, 65
boxing, 167
Bradley Air Museum tornado damage, Windsor Locks, 115
Bradley Field, Windsor Locks, 115
Brainard Field dedication, 24
Branford, 28–29, 110
Bray, Chris, 52
breakdancing, 62
Breuer, Marcel, 36
Bridges, 6-7, 13, 15, 23, 26, 39, 181
Bristol, 113
Brooklyn, Connecticut, hanging in, 123
Brooklyn Market, 25
Brooks, Joel, 151
Brown, Daniel, 69
Brown, John, 95
Brown v. Board of Education, 94
Brownie Troop 61 in Memorial Day Parade, 47
Brubeck, Dave, 161
Brunton, Richard, 122
Buell, Abel, 122
Bulkeley, Morgan, 81
Burns Elementary School Brownies, 47
Bush, George W., 91
Bushnell, David, 69
Bushnell, Rev. Horace, 18
Bushnell Memorial Hall, 146–47
Bushnell Park, 13, 15, 49

C. H. Dexter & Sons saw and grist mill, Windsor Locks, 185
Cafe Beauregard, New Britain, 91
Calder, Alexander, 159
Calhoun, Jim, 174
Camp Courant, 45
Cannon, Sharice, 105
cannon made in Salisbury, 184
capital punishment, 123-126, 131, 132
Capitol Building

on 350th Anniversary, 38
    about, 38
    dome construction, 12
    Electoral College voting, 90
    General Assembly's opening day, 84
    Hall of the House, 78–79
    views of, 15, 26
    Youth Services budget cuts protest, 86
Cardoso, Jorge, 34
Casper, Billy, 180
Cathedral of St. Joseph fire, 138
Cayne, Carli, 55
Centennial Parade, Windsor Locks, 46
Center Congregational Church, 16
Central Connecticut State University, 177
Cervoni, Kayla, 65
Chabad House of the Valley, Simsbury, 56
Chapman, Gerald, 125
Chapman, Johanna Petit, 132
"Charles Goodyear" (Healy), 185
Charter Oak, 79
Charter Oak Bridge opening, 26
Charter Oak Cultural Center, 63
Charter Oak Landing, fishing at, 27
Charter Oak Park, 167
Checketts, Gabe, 145
Checketts, Will, 145
Cheney Silk Mills, 189
Cheshire, First Congregational Church, 143
Cheshire High School girls' swim team, 178
Christensen, Marit, 170
Christmas, 55, 57
Church, Frederic Edwin, 9, 157
Churchill, Elijah, 69
"Ciona" (Pilobolus Dance Theater), 162
civil unions, 102
Civil War, *front cover,* 66–67, 70, 71, 136
Clark, Seth H., 8
classical music, 147, 160
Clay, Edward Williams, 10
Clean Water Act of Connecticut, 31
Clemens, Clara, 22
Clemens, Jean, 22
Clemens, Livy, 22
Clemens, Samuel "Mark Twain," 22, 153
Clemens, Susy, 22
Clemens residence, 22

Clinton, Bill, 91
Clinton, Morgan High School, 179
clockworks, 186
Cohen Farms, Ellington, 34
Colchester, InCord factory, 60
Collinsville, Farmington River, 31
Colt, Elizabeth, 155
Colt, Samuel, 187
Colt's Patent Firearms Manufacturing Co., 182–83, 187
community, 40–65
Conant, Brittney, 178
Condon, Charles, 85
Connecticut
    350th Anniversary, 38
    as "Arsenal of Democracy," 67
    history of, 41, 79
    as "Provision State," 67
    as slave state, 93
Connecticut Agricultural College athletics, 173, 174
Connecticut Airport Authority (CAA), 201
Connecticut Courant, The, 3, 14, 32. *See also* Hartford Courant, The
Connecticut Historical Society, 194
Connecticut Office of Tourism, 202
Connecticut River, 6-7, 8, 108, 181
Connecticut Science Center, 27, 64, 199
Connecticut Sportsmen's and Boat Show, 47
"Connecticut Yankee in King Arthur's Court" (Twain), 183
Considine, Erin, 141
cookbook, first in the United States, 185
Cosey Beach storm damage, 116, 118
Coventry, Nathan Hale Homestead, 32
Coventry High School volleyball team, 178
Coy, George, 188
Cozza, Carm, 177
Crafts, Richard B., 128
Crandall, Audrey M., 50
Crandall, Prudence, 92, 93, 94
crime, 120–33
    about, 129–32
    Chapman, Gerald, 125
    counterfeiters, 122
    Crafts, Richard B., 128
    and death penalty, 123-126, 131, 132
    Grasso, William "The Wild Guy," 127
    hangings, 123

Petit family murders, 132, 143
    politics and prison, 79
    Sandy Hook Elementary School shooting, 120–21, 133, 144, 145
Cronin, John, 123
"Crowbar Governor, The," 81
Cybalski tobacco farm, Enfield, 42

D

dance, 162–63
Daniel, Jesrene, 77
"Daniel Wadsworth" (Sully), 11
Deane, Silas, 68
death penalty, 123, 124, 125, 126, 131, 132
DECD Connecticut Office of Tourism, 202
Declaration of Independence, 80
Dederer, DeeAnna, 102
deforestation vs. conservation in 1817, 32
Demanosow, Allison, 141
demonstrations
    anti-Vietnam War, 75
    death penalty protest, 131
    income tax protest, 88
    race related, 98, 99, 100, 101
    for suffrage, 96
    Youth Services budget cuts protest, 86
Derby, Housatonic River dam, 31
Detrick, Bill, 177
Detter, Johan, 177
Diaz, Kendrick, 57
Dickenson, Dave, 172
Dineen, Kevin, 172
"Dinosaurs Alive" 3D movie premier, 64
disasters. *See* fires; tragedies; weather
Dodd, Christopher J., 84
Dodge, Alexander, 151
"Domestic Economy" (Webster), 32
Drake, Samuel Adams, 8
Dropo, Walt, 171
Drury, Chris, 171
Duerling, Mary Ann, 191
Dura Biotech, 191
Durang, Christopher, 150

E

East Haddam, Goodspeed Opera House, 149
East Hartford, 6–7, 55, 63
East Lyme High School Viking Marching Band, 49

East Windsor, Windsorville Post Office, 50
Easter, 54, 55
Easter vigil, Metropolitan A.M.E. Zion
    Church, 54
Ebner, Brez, 140
Eddy Farm, Newington, 34
Edwards, Olayinka, 65
Egan, John, 171
El-Amin, Khalid, 174
Electoral College, 90
Ellington, Cohen Farms, 34
Ellington, Duke, 161
"Emigration of Hooker and His Party to
    Hartford" (Clark), 8
Enfield, 42
equal rights, 92–103
    about, 93, 94–95
    gay rights, 93, 102–3
    race and equality, 92, 93, 94, 95,
        98–101
    suffrage, 93, 96, 97, 123
Evans, Gregory, 162
Everett, Rev. Walter, 142
Expeditionary Learning Academy, Moylan
    School, 63

F

"Face Value" (Padberg), 62
Fales & Gray Car Works explosion, 136
Fall foliage, cover, 32, 33
Farmington River, Collinsville, 31
Farrah, Alexander, 64
Farrah, Spencer, 64
Fenwick cottage of Hepburns, 110
Fidlar, Charles, 160
Fiesta del Norte band members, 63
Figliomeni, Vincent, 139
fires, 101, 135-138, *back cover*
"First Company Governor's Foot Guard"
    lithograph (Kellogg and Kellogg), 10
First Congregational Church, Cheshire,
    143
fishing, 27, 31
Fitch, Mike, 172
Flanagan, Catherine, 96, 97
floods
    1692, 105
    1936, 108, 109
    1955, *front cover*, 112, 113
Flores, Hugo, 34
Foley Farm, Simsbury, 32
football, 168–69, 173, 179

Foote, Hallie, 151
Foote, Horton, 151
Forestville after Blizzard of 1888, 106
Founders Bridge, 181
"Four Saints in Three Acts" (Stein and
    Thomson), 155
Fowler, Douglass, 71
Francis, Ron, 172
Frazer, Mackenzie, 61
Friedland, Bruce, 56
"Frogs, The" (Yale Repertory Theatre),
    150
Fuentes, Nidia, 55
Fuller, Aldred C., 23
Fuller, Nancy, 46
Fuller Brush Company, The, 23
Fundamental Orders of Connecticut, 79

G

G. Fox & Co. department store, 21, 51
Gala at the Club at Rentscher Field, East
    Hartford, 63
Ganim, Joseph P., 79, 89
Gareau, Larry, 63
gay rights, 93, 102–3
geese, 35
Gerber, H. Joseph, 191
Gerena, Victor Manuel, 129
Giardina, Dave, 63
Gillette, William, 148
Ginsburg, Harry, 126
"Giselle" (ballet), 163
Glass House, New Canaan, 36
Goldman, Samuel, 54
golf, 180
Goodspeed, William, 149
Goodspeed Opera House, East Haddam,
    149
Goodwin, Rev. Francis, 18
Goodwin Park, 19, 24
Goodyear, Charles, 185
Gores, Landis, 36
Grant, Donald, 52
Grant's store, 98
Grasso, Ella, 79, 84
Grasso, William "The Wild Guy," 127
"Gravity of Color, The" (Hoke), 159
Green, Thomas, 3, 7
Green Street Arts Center, Middletown, 61
Griffin, Christine, 48
Griffin, Donald, Jr., 48

Grippo, Joe, 179
Griswold, Florence, 157
Griswold, Matthew, 122
Gulf War and Gulf War Syndrome, 68

H

Hale Homestead, Coventry, 32
Hall of the House, Capitol Building,
    78–79
Hamden, 104–5, 115, 116
Hamill, Dorothy, 171
Hamilton, Richard, 174
Hanna, Lucille, 48
"Hard Winter of 1780," 106
Harder, Lee, 55
Hardy, George, 48
Harris, Sarah, 94
Harrison, Jordan, 134–35
Hartford
    and Flood of 1936, 108, 109
    history of, 7, 10, 15
    "rain of parks," 18
    See also Hartford street scenes
Hartford Chiefs, 166
Hartford Courant, The
    about, 3
    on Archer Home as murder factory,
        124
    on Beck executions, 130
    and Declaration of Independence, 80
    on fire on "day of general rejoicing,"
        135
    on Gillette as Sherlock Holmes, 148
    on Harrison inauguration, 80
    on Kennedy assassination, 83
    on Lincoln assassination, 80
    on Ross, 131
    on Sandy Hook school shooting, 133
    on September 11, 2001, terrorist
        attacks, 134–35, 140, 141
    on Stevens, 154
    and Webster, 152
    See also Connecticut Courant, The
Hartford Covered Bridge, 6
Hartford Dark Blues, 166
Hartford Hospital, 44, 136, 197
Hartford Ladies Cycle Club, 17
Hartford National Bank Building, 24
Hartford Public High School students,
    100
Hartford street scenes

Asylum Street, 4, 21
    Flower Street, 23
    Front Street, 25, 108
    Gold Street, 21
    Lawrence and Grant streets, 119
    Main Street, 16, 21, 24, 107
    "Perfect Sixes" on Park Terrace, 36
    Temple Street, 108
    Trumbull and Pearl streets, 108
Hartford Symphony Orchestra, 63, 160
Hartley, Bria, 164–65
Harvey, Anthony, 148
Harvey, Matt, 179
Hawke, MaryBelle, 132, 142
Hawke, Rev. Richard, 132, 142
Hawthorn Farm, Enfield, 42
Hayden, Rev. Herbert, 122
Hayden, Rosa, 122
Hayes, T. Frank, 79, 89
Health Center, UConn, Farmington, 193
Healy, George Peter Alexander, 185
heat wave, summer of 1911, 108
Hebron Harvest Fair, 52
Heck, Bill, 151
Hellwig, Tracy, 55
Hennessy, Minnie, 96
Henwood, Mary, 141
Hepburn, Katharine, *front cover*, 110,
    148
Hernandez, Blanca, 60
Hickey, Edward J., 125
Higganum, Bogue Farms, 35
Hill-Stead Museum, 159
Hoke, Lisa, 159
Holmstead, Molly, 145
Holtz, Skip, 173
Hooker, Thomas, 7, 8, 9
Hooker residence, 8
"Hooker's Company Reach the
    Connecticut" (Drake), 8
Hopkins, John Jay, 82
hospital, need for, 136. *See also* Hartford
    Hospital
"Hot Air Club" of impressionist painters,
    157
Housatonic River dam, Derby, 31
Howe, Gordie, 172
Howe, Mark, 172
Howe, Marty, 172

Hunt, Karen, 160
Hurlock, Matt, 178
hurricanes
    1635, 105
    1815, 106
    Connie and Diane, 113
    damage from, 110, 111
    Sandy, 116, 118
hygiene exercise at South Manchester
    Open-Air School, 45
Hynes, Carolyne, 141
Hynes, Olivia, 141

I

ice hockey, 172
income tax debates and protests, 88
InCord factory, Colchester, 60
industrialization/manufacturing, 184, 186,
    187, 190
ingenuity. *See* innovation
Inhphom, Erick, 62
innovation, 182–93
    about, 183, 193
    bicycles, telephones, and typewriters,
        188
    Cheney Silk Mills, 189
    Colt's Patent Arms Manufacturing Co.,
        182–83, 187
    interchangeable parts, 186
    machine age, 187
interchangeable parts, 186
Iraq War, 68, 76
Irish immigrants, discrimination against,
    93
iron mining, 184
Ives, Charles, 160
Ivins, Bruce E., 130

J

Jackson Laboratory, The, 193
Jacob Strong Homestead, Torrington, 36
jazz music, 161
Jefferson, Moriah, 164–65
Jenner, Bruce, 170
Jeresaty, Cathie, 64
Jeresaty, Robert, 64
Johansen, John, 36
"John Butler Talcott" (Chase), 159
Johnson, Arne, 129
Johnson, Lyndon Baines, 83, *back cover*
Johnson, Philip, 36
Johnson, William, 68

Jones, Myra, 59
Jones, Paul, 59
Joyce, Joan, 170
Joyce D. and Andrew J. Mandell
    Academy for Teachers, 199
J.R. Loan Company, 25
Julian, John, 161

K

Karmanos, Peter, 172
Katharine Hepburn Cultural Arts Center,
    Old Saybrook, 148
Keeney, Cliff, 166
Kellogg, E.B. & E.C., 10, 11, 71
Kelly, Alex, 130
Kelly, Emmett, 137
Kennedy, John F., 79, 83
Kerrigan, Beth, 103
Kesselring, Joseph, 124
Kiely, Arthur J., Jr., 72
Kimball, Dan A., 82
King, Martin Luther, Jr., 98, 100
Knapp, Vera, 140
Knights of Columbus, 87
Know-Nothing movement, 79
Kolpa, Marjorie J., 126
Korean War, 73
Kosswig, Ernest, *front cover*, 113
Krieble, Vernon, 191
Krieger, Jeff, 160
Kuan, Carolyn, 63

L

Labieniec, Stanley, 126
Lacy, Maggie, 151
L'Ambiance Plaza collapse, 139
landscape, 28–39
    about, 29, 31, 32
    agriculture, 34, 35, 42
    architecture, 32, 36–39
    Swan Beach, Long Island Sound, 30
    Washburn Preserve, 28–29
    See also rivers; scenic views
Lanza, Adam, 121, 133, 145
Lathrop, Tiffany, 178
Lauray, Betty Lynn, 58
Lavery, Peter, funeral of, 142
Lawler, Rachel, 131
Lee, Ezra, 69
Lee, Henry, 128
Leetch, Brian, 171

Lemon, Meadowlark, 171
Lenthe, Ed, 166
Lester, Garner, 140
Levitow, John Lee, 74
LeWitt, Sol, 156–57
Lights of Hope for Petit family, First
    Congregational Church, Cheshire, 143
Lilly, Kristine, 170, 171
Lincoln, Abraham, 71, 80,
literature, 151, 152–54
Little, Floyd, 171
"Living Creche," Bloomfield United
    Methodist Church, 57
Lobo, Rebecca, 176
Lockyer, Victoria, 102
Loctite, 191
log-rolling contest, 47
London's Barber Shop, 25
"Long Day's Journey Into Night" (O'Neill),
    154
Long Island Sound, Swan Beach, Old
    Lyme, 30
Love, Rev. William De Loss, Jr., 18
Lundgren, Ottilie, death from anthrax
    poisoning, 130
Lux Bond & Green, 198
Lyme Art Colony, 157
Lynds, Clyde, 26

M
MacArthur, Kathleen, 52
Macheteros, Los, 129
machine age, 187
Maerz, Robert, 191
Malhotra, Vikram, 177
Malloy, Dannel, 91
Manchester Road Race, 53
Mansfield, Shundahi Farm, 34
manufacturing, 184, 186, 187, 190
map of the United States by Buell, 122
March on Washington, 99
Marquez-Greene, Nelba, 145
Martin, Jane Scichili, 162
Martino, Olivia, 65
Matthews, Frank, 114
Matthews, Roberta, 114
Max's Oyster Bar, West Hartford, 60
McBarron, H. Charles, 69
McDonnell, Chris, 120–21
McDonnell, Lynn, 120–21
McDonough, Thomas F., 126

McDonough Hotel, Middletown, 106
McLean, Jackie, 161
M.D. Fox School students, 49
Mello, Argarito, 63
Meshomasic State Forest, Portland, 32
Meskill, Thomas J., 84
Metropolitan A.M.E. Zion Church Easter
    vigil, 54
Middlefield, Powder Ridge Music Festival,
    161
Middletown, 39, 61, 106, 111
Miller, Scott, 60
Mills, Nicole, 178
Milner, Thirman, 99
Minor, William T., 79
Misko, Barbara, 55
Misko, Bill, 55
Misko, Mike, 55
Mock, Jody, 103
Moore, Maya, 176
Morgan, J.P., and Wadsworth Atheneum
    Museum of Art, 155
Morgan High School, Clinton, 179
Morrone, Joe, 177
Mortensen, William, 160
Mortensen Riverfront Plaza, Riverfront
    Dragon Boat and Asian Festival, 63
Mosqueda-Lewis, Kaleena, 164–65
Mount Olive Baptist Church
    groundbreaking ceremonies, 98
Moylan School, Expeditionary Learning
    Academy, 63
Murphy, Calvin, 170
music, 49, 147, 160, 161
Myren, Eric, 177

N
Napier, Shabazz, 175
Nathan Hale Homestead, Coventry, 32
National Prisoner of War Museum,
    Andersonville, Georgia, 71
NECAP (North End Community Action
    Project) rally, 99
New Britain, 190
New Britain Museum of American Art,
    158–59
New Canaan, Glass House, 36
New England Telephone Co., 188
New Haven Green, protests about "New
    Haven Nine," 101
New London and 1815 hurricane, 106
Newington, Eddy Farm, 34

Newington Police Officer Peter Lavery,
    142
Newman, Paul, 150
Newsome, Arkeel, 179
Niemis, Stella, 85
North End Community Action Project
    (NECAP) rally, 99
Norwich and 1815 hurricane, 106
Nowobilski , Harry, 55
Nowobilski , Stasia, 55
Noyes, Eliot, 36
Nutcracker productions, 63, 162

O
Obama, Barack, 79, 91
Occuish, Hannah, 123
Okafor, Emeka, 174
Old Lyme, 30, 110
"Old New-Gate Prison" engraving
    (Brunton), 122
Old Saybrook, Katharine Hepburn Cultural
    Arts Center, 148
Old State House, 7, 10, 24, 26.
"Old State House" (Clay), 10
O'Neill, Eugene, 154
opera, 149, 160
"Orphans' Home Cycle" (Foote), 151
Ortiz, Ginna, 133
Our Lady of Fatima Church, 54

P
Padberg, Carol, 62
painters, 156–57
Palmer, Arnold, 180
Palmer, Richard, 103
parades
    East Lyme High School Viking
        Marching Band in, 49
    high-wheel bicycles in, 16
    Memorial Day Parade, 47
    "Votes for Women" suffrage parade,
        Hartford, 97
    Windsor Locks Centennial Parade, 46
Paranov, Moshe, 160
Parasol, Peter, 154
Park River
    about, 31
    diversion, 13
    and Hurricane of 1938, 111
    ice skating on, 20
    and Soldiers and Sailors Memorial
        Arch, 13

views of, 13, 15
Park Terrace, "Perfect Sixes" on, 36
parks
    Bushnell Park, 13, 15, 49
    Goodwin Park, 19, 24
    Pope Park, 18
    "rain of parks," 18
    Sherwood Island State Park, 141
    Wickham Park, front cover, 33
Parone, Edward, 154
Pastomerlo, Jane, 46
Paternostro, Christina, 139
Patriarca, Raymond L.S., 127
Patrick, Deval, 91
Paul, Alice, 96
Paulsen, Lee, 146
P.C. Richard & Son, 196
Pep, Willie, 167, 170
peach trees, 34
Pennington, James W.C., 95
Perez, Thomas, 91
"Perfect Sixes" on Park Terrace, 36
Perry, Horace B., 122
Petit, William J., Jr., 132
Petit family murders, 132, 143
Phoenix Company "Boat Building," 37
Pieczarka, William, 134–35
Piersall, Jimmy, 171
Pilobolus Dance Theater, 162
Police Department, 16, 43, 142
politics, 78–91
    "Black Law," 94
    Fundamental Orders of Connecticut,
        79
    and prison, 79
    suffrage, 93, 96, 97, 123
    See also demonstrations; voters and
        voting; specific politicians
pollution, dealing with, 31
Pope, Albert, 16, 43, 188
Pope, Theodate, 159
Pope-Hartford police patrol van, 16
Pope Manufacturing Co., 188
Pope Park, 18
Portland, Meshomasic State Forest, 32
Portuguese folk-dancing group (Rancho
    Folclarico de Hartford), 54
Potter, John, 148
Powder Ridge Music Festival, Middlefield,
    161
Pratt & Whitney Co., 23, 190

produce carts on Front Street, 25
"Prompter, The" (Webster), 152
"Provision State" in Revolutionary War, 67
Prudence Crandall's school for colored
    girls, 92, 94
pumpkins, 34
Purim service, Chabad House of the
    Valley, Simsbury, 56
Putnam, Israel, 69
"Putnam Leaving the Plow" (Kellogg &
    Bulkeley), 69
Putting Down Roots children's organic
    gardening program, 63

Q
"Quenticut" (Lynds), 26

R
race and equality
    about, 93
    and Brown, 95
    and Crandall's school for colored girls,
        92, 94
    demonstrations, 98, 99, 100, 101
    and King, 98, 100
    Pennington's ministry, 95
Rackley, Alex, 101
"Radio Golf" (Wilson), 151
"rain of parks," 18
Rancho Folclarico de Hartford
    (Portuguese folk-dancing group), 54
Rathbun, Terry, 76
Reagan, Ronald, 87
Real Art Ways, 62
Reardon, George, 129
recovery, 135. See also tragedies
Red Cross, Hepburn and, front cover
Reid, Ray, 177
Rell, M. Jodi, 78–79
Remigino, Lindy, 171
Rentschler, Frederick, 190
Revolutionary War, 67, 68, 69
Ribicoff, Abraham A., 84, 126
Riege, Steve, 131
Rieger, Chris Lux, 162
Riley, John, 160
Ringling Bros. and Barnum & Bailey
    Circus big top fire, 137, back cover
River Ridge, Avon, 59

Rivera, Joshua, 134–35
Riverfront Dragon Boat and Asian Festival,
    Mortensen Riverfront Plaza, 63
Riverfront Plaza, 26
Riverfront Rowing Regatta, 181
rivers, 31, See also Connecticut River,
    Park River
Rizzotti, Jennifer, 171
Roark, Matt, 52
Robinette, Michelle, 91
Robinson, O.P., 82
Robustelli, Andy, 170
Rocco, Brandon, 65
Rodgers, Bill, 171
Rogers Orchards, Southington, 34
roller skating on Capitol grounds, 51
Roman Catholic prelates, 87
Roosevelt, Franklin Delano, 81
Roosevelt, Theodore, 43, 79
Ross, Michael, 131
rowing, 181
Rowland, John G., 79, 89, 169
Royal typewriters, 188
Rozinsky, Simon, 54
Russell, Rosalind, 149
Ruth, Babe, 166

S
Saint Francis Care, 203
Salihou, Nafissa, 65
Salisbury and iron mining/manufacturing,
    184
same-sex marriage, 93, 102–3
Samuels, Rabbi Mendel, 56
Sandy Hook Elementary School shooting,
    120–21, 133, 144, 145
Santopietro, Joseph, 79
Santos, Andres, 134–35
Savitt, Bill, 166
scenic views
    Arrigoni Bridge, 39
    Charter Oak Landing, 27
    Connecticut Science Center, 27
    "Emigration of Hooker and His Party to
        Hartford" (Clark), 8
    Farmington River, 31
    Foley Farm, 32
    Goodwin Park, 19
    Hartford, 15
    Hartford skyline from Wickham Park,
        front cover, 33
    "Hooker's Company Reach the

Connecticut" (Drake), 8
Housatonic River dam, 31
Meshomasic State Forest, 32
Nathan Hale Homestead, 32
Park River and Soldiers and Sailors
    Memorial Arch, 13
"Reverend Thomas Hooker and
    Company..." (Church), 9
Riverfront Plaza, 26
Swan Beach, Long Island Sound, 30
"The View of Hartford as Seen from
    East Hartford," 6–7
Washburn Preserve, 28–29
    See also Hartford street scenes; street
    scenes
Schand, Chevon, 58
Schand, Shamel Lateek, 58
Schulz, Ally, 65
"Sea God of Magic, The" (play), 155
Seale, Bobby, 101
Seguro, Olinda, 54
Sept. 11, 2001, terrorist attacks,
    134–35, 140, 141
Sereno, Lori, 178
Sharma, Parth, 177
Shelley, Edwin, 131
Shelley, Lera, 131
Sherman, Clifton L., 124
Sherwood Island State Park, 141
Shiloh Baptist Church, 58
Shundahi Farm, Mansfield, 34
"Signing Santa Day," Westfarms Mall, 57
Sikorsky, Igor, 191
"Silas Deane" (Johnson), 68
Silvester, Paul, 79
Simmons, Amelia, 185
Simsbury, 32.56
Sirois, Eric, 191
Sister Rose, 52
Sisters of Saint Joseph of Chambéry,
    203
Smedley Company, 43
Smith, Abby, 123
Smith, Julia, 123
Smith, Rabbi Moshe, 56
snow storms/blizzards, 104–5, 106,
    107, 116, 117, 119, back cover
soccer, 170, 177
Soldiers and Sailors Memorial Arch, 13
Sommariva, Kelly, 178
Sousa, Emma, 178
South Manchester Open-Air School, 45

Southern New England Telephone Co.
    switchboard, 188
Southington, 34, 107
sports, 164–81
    about, 165, 170–71
    baseball, 165, 166, 179
    basketball, 164–65, 171, 174-177
    boxing, 167
    fishing, 27, 31
    football, 168–69, 173, 177, 179
    golf, 180
    hockey, 172
    roller skating, 51
    rowing, 181
    soccer, 170, 177
    squash, 177
    swimming, 30, 178
    track and field, 33, 170
    volleyball, 178, 179
Springsteen, Bruce, 161
squash, 177
St. Francis Hospital, 44, 203
St. John's Episcopal Church, Newtown,
    144
St. Joseph's Residence, 52
Stamford, "Boomerang!" shot in, 149
Stanizzi, Frances, 73
Stanizzi, James, 73
Stanley Works, New Britain, 190
Stannard, Mary, 122
state house. See Capitol Building, Old
    State House
Steele, Bob, and Babe Ruth, 166
"Stegosaurus" (Calder), 159
Stein, Gertrude, 155
Stevens, Wallace, 153–54
Stewart, Breanna, 176
Stiefel, Milton, 148
Still, Chuck, 148
Stock, Adrian, 60
Stokes, Kiah, 164–65
Stone, Rev. Samuel, 7
Stonington and 1815 hurricane, 106
Stop & Shop at Bristol Plaza, 47
Stowe, Harriet Beecher, 93, 147,
    152–53
Stratford, Vought-Sikorsky Aircraft Corp.,
    191
Streep, Meryl, 150, 151
street scenes
    Main Street, Bristol, 113

Main Street, East Hartford, 55
Main Street, Southington, 107
Main Street, Winsted, 112
    See also Hartford street scenes; scenic
    views
Strong, Ken, 171
submarines, 69, 82
suffrage, 93, 96, 97, 123
Sully, Thomas, 11
summer of 1911 heat wave, 108
Swan Beach, Long Island Sound, Old
    Lyme, 30
swimming, 30, 178

T
Taborsky, Joseph "Mad Dog," 126
Talcott, John Butler, 159
Talley, Michael, 160
Taylor, Jerome, 57
Taylor, Larry, 173
"Tchaikovsky Pas de Deux" (Balanchine),
    162
telephones, 188
terrorist attacks, September 11, 2001,
    134–35, 140, 141
Terry, Eli, 186
"Thirteen Ways Of Looking At A
    Blackbird" (Stevens), 154
Theater, 147-151
Thompson, Harry, 76
Thomson, Virgil, 155
3D movie, 64
tobacco, 42
Torah procession, 54
torching of Prudence Crandall's school,
    The Anti-Slavery Almanac, 92, 94
tornadoes, 106, 114, 115
Torres, Juan, 34
Torrington, Jacob Strong Homestead, 36
track and field, 170
tragedies, 134–45
    about, 135
    dump truck collision with bus and
        cars, 142
    Fales & Gray Car Works explosion,
        136
    L'Ambiance Plaza collapse, 139
    Newington Police Officer Peter Lavery
        killed in the line of duty, 142
    Sandy Hook Elementary School
        shooting, 120–21, 133, 144, 145
    Sept. 11, 2001, terrorist attacks,

134–35, 140, 141
    See also crime; fires; weather
Travelers Tower, 26, 27, 37
Trinity College, 177, 192
trolleys, 24
Tropical Storm Irene, 116
Tross, David, 77
Truman, Harry S., 82
Twain, Mark, 22, 153, 183
Twain residence, 22
"Turtle" submarine, 69
Twain, Mark, 22, 153, 183
typewriters, 188

U
UConn, The Jackson Laboratory, at the
    Health Center, Farmington, 193
UConn athletics
    basketball, 164–65, 174-177
    football, 173, 179
    soccer, 170, 177
"Uncle Tom's Cabin" (Stowe), 93, 147,
    152–53
Underwood typewriters, 188
Unionville and Flood of 1955, 113
Upjohn, Richard M., 38
U.S. Coast Guard Academy, 91
U.S. Postal Service's Hepburn stamp,
    148
USS Nautilus (submarine), 82

V
Valentine, Bobby, 171
Valentine's Day, renewing vows on, 59
Vaslett, Victoria, 162
Vaughn, Mo, 171
Vazquez, Juan, 55
Vazquez, Yadira, 55
Vietnam War, 74, 75
"View of Hartford as Seen from East
    Hartford, The" (A.R.W.), 6–7
Villa, Milton, 134–35
Vincent, Debbie, 51
volleyball, 178, 179
voters and voting
    Electoral College, 90
    machines for, 85
    minorities, 93
    suffrage, 93, 96, 97, 123
Vought-Sikorsky Aircraft Corp., Stratford,
    191

W
Wadsworth, Daniel, 11
"Wadsworth Atheneum, The," lithograph
    (Kellogg and Kellogg), 11
Wadsworth Atheneum Museum of Art,
    155–57
Walker, Kemba, 174
"Wall Drawing #1131, Whirls and Twirls
    (Wadsworth)" (LeWitt), 156–57
Wallingford tornado of 1878, 106
war and valor, 66–77
    22nd Connecticut Volunteers, 71
    26th Regiment soldiers, front cover,
        66–67
    192nd Military Police Battalion of
        Niantic, 77
    about, 67–69, 74
    "First Company Governor's Foot Guard"
        lithograph, 10
    prisoners of war, 71
    Soldiers and Sailors Memorial Arch, 13
    See also specific wars
War in Afghanistan, 68
Washburn Preserve, Branford, 28–29
Wasley, Donna, 85
Wasley, Robin, 85
Wasp engine, Pratt & Whitney Co., 190
Waterbury and Flood of 1955, 113
Waterston, Sam, 148
Watkins, Oliver, 123
Watson, Bubba, 180
Watson, Ebenezer, 80
Watson, Madeline, 97
weather, 104–19
    floods, front cover, 105, 108, 109,
        112, 113
    heat wave, 108
    snow storms/blizzards, 104–5, 106,
        107, 116, 117, 119, back cover
    tornadoes, 106, 114, 115
    Tropical Storm Irene, 116
    See also hurricanes
weather balloon launch, 115
Weatherbee, Lorraine, 46
Weaver, Sigourney, 150
Webster, Noah, 32, 152
wedding, Schand and Lauray, 58
Weed, Helena Hill, 96
Weed Sewing Machine Co., 23
Weicker, Lowell P., Jr., 88
Weinstein, Andy, 116

Weinstein, Shayna, 116
Welles, Gideon, 71
West Hartford, 46, 60
Westbrook and Tropical Storm Irene, 116
Westfarms Mall "Signing Santa Day," 57
Whalers, 172
Whedon, Bill, 180
White, Henry, on Wadsworth Atheneum
    Museum of Art, 155
White Sand Beach hurricane damage,
    Old Lyme, 110
Whitehead, Gustave, 190
Whitney, Eli, 186
Wickham Park, Hartford skyline from,
    front cover, 33
Williamson, John, 171
Wilson, August, 151
Windsor, tornado damage in, 114
Windsor High School graduation, 65
Windsor Locks, 46, 115, 185
Windsor Market, 100
Windsorville Post Office, East Windsor, 50
Winsted, 112
winter, "Hard Winter of 1780," 106
winter of "The Great Snow," 1717, 105
Winter Solstice Celebration, Green Street
    Arts Center, Middletown, 61
Winthrop, John, Jr. (The Younger), 79,
    184
Wojculewicz, Frank, 126
Women's League, 45
women's right to vote, 93
wood chipper murder, 128
Woodward, Joanne, 150
World War I, 67
World War II, 67–68, 72

Y
Yale
    Bollingen Prize for Poetry, 154
    chaplain William Sloane Coffin, 121
    first black student, 95
    football, 168, 177
    Repertory Theatre productions, 150,
        151
    squash, 177
Yanez, Samantha, 178
Young, Steve, 170
Youth Services budget cuts protest, 86

Z
Zysk, Billy, 52